# MOUNT SHASTA . . .
## *Where Heaven and Earth Meet*

# Contents

## About the Editors . . .

**Jane English** grew up in a small town in New England and graduated from Mount Holyoke College. She began photographing professionally in her mid-twenties after completing a Ph.D. in physics at the University of Wisconsin and then decided not to continue with a science career. Her black and white photographs of nature illustrate six books, including a best-selling translation of the Chinese classic *Tao Te Ching*, published in 1972 by Random House. Her other interests include gardening, skiing, amateur radio and hot air ballooning.

Her own publishing business, Earth Heart, began in 1985 with the publication of her book, *Different Doorway: Adventures of a Caesarean Born*. She moved Earth Heart to Mount Shasta in 1987 and for six years published *The Mount Shasta Calendar*, using black-and-white and color photographs by several photographers. This book grows out of the calendars and expands her vision of the mountain as a common reference point.

**Jenny Coyle** came to know the back country of California through Girl Scouting. It was her childhood wish that one day she could make her home in the mountains. In 1983 she graduated with a degree in journalism from California Polytechnic State University in San Luis Obispo, and her first job was with a small chain of weekly newspapers at the foot of Mount Shasta. Her first glimpse of the mountain, from 100 miles away, told her that her wish had come true.

She continued to write for the newspaper chain for 10 years before leaving that job to work on independent writing projects. Her work has appeared in the San Francisco Chronicle, the L.A. Weekly, the Redding Record Searchlight, and Siskiyou Best of Times.

Her interests include world travel, hiking and skiing, reading, community dynamics, and potlucks.

Jenny's years of experience covering Mount Shasta-area news gave her the perspective and knowledge of the community needed to edit this book.

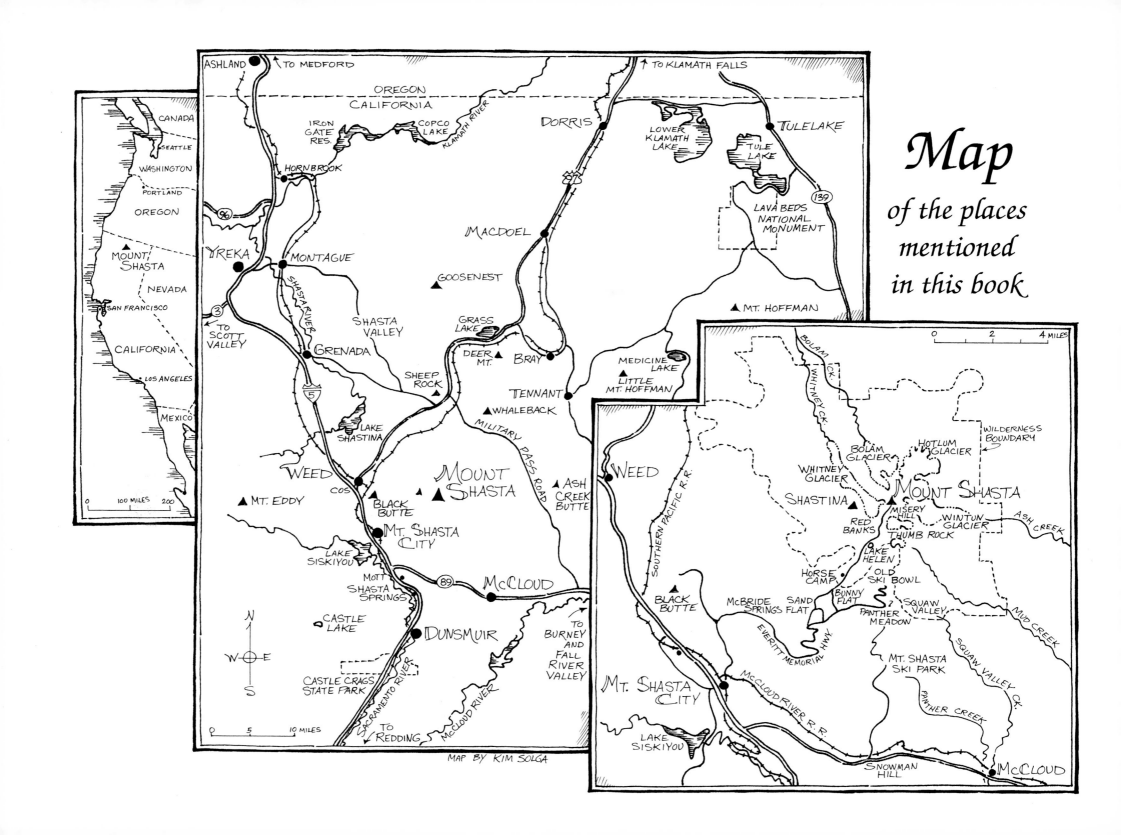

Map

of the places mentioned in this book

MAP BY KIM SOLGA

From the North

From the West

From the South

From the East

7

# Preface

There is a difference between knowing the sun will rise, and actually crawling out of bed in the early dawn to watch waves of watermelon and tangerine sweep across a still-starlit sky.

This book has been that experience for me. After working for nearly a dozen years as a journalist in Siskiyou County, I knew in my mind that Mount Shasta does not mean the same thing, or serve the same purpose, for all people. It was not until I queried 44 of them on their feelings for this mountain that I understood with my heart the depth—and worth—of each perspective.

The writings in this book are meant to present outlooks on Mount Shasta that are shared by many, many people. At the same time, I am keenly aware that not every perspective is represented.

My own relationship with the mountain is about women climbers, and my admiration for them: for Olive Paddock Eddy, the first pioneer woman known to reach the summit, in 1856, in the days when women climbed in skirts and used soot as sunscreen; for Kerry Moran, my first Shasta climbing partner who has since moved to Nepal; for my mother, Debbie Coyle, who climbed at age 56; for my stepdaughter, Sierra, who reached the summit at age 15; for Suzanne Wilkins, a friend who fulfilled a lifelong dream when she scrambled onto the peak at 14,162 feet; for my best friend Darcy Aston, who climbed Shasta for the first time one month before beginning the adventure of a marriage; for the ballerina I met whose leg muscles and discipline put her on top well ahead of her father and brother; and for all of those who have been on the annual women's climb organized by Linda Chitwood and I, many of whom have had to overcome great fear even to strap on a pair of crampons and learn to use an ice axe.

Maybe you will see yourself in this book. It is my hope that every reader will make a sincere effort to understand the points of view presented here, and then cherish the beauty of our differences.

— *Jenny Coyle,* September 1995

*The mountain is something all of us in this community have in common. Though our approaches to it and relationships with it are many and diverse-- hiking, downhill skiing, mountaineering, cross-country skiing, meditating, photographing, logging, communing with spiritual entities, promoting tourism and development, appreciating its beauty, studying its geology and history, and just being aware of its presence. But there is something about the mountain that also unifies us all. This something is not only the physical mountain of rock, snow, and trees, but also its inner reflection or resonance, an inmost place within each of us that is best not named. Because it is in the naming that our differences arise. If we can act from this sense of deep inner oneness that our mountain reminds us of, then our differences, rather than being fragmented, conflicting interests, will shine as multiple facets of a single jewel.*

The above paragraph served as a statement of purpose during the six years I created and published the Mount Shasta Calendar. This book is a natural outgrowth of the calendars, giving sixty-nine writers and photographers a place to give their diverse perspectives on Mount Shasta, and show the common ground we all share.

I find it a delight to create something as beautiful as this book. I hope the final product is also a delight to you the reader.

— *Jane English,* September, 1995

---

## Acknowledgements

Without the help and support of our friends and families this book would not have happened. There are many who helped; they know who they are.

*In particular, Jane thanks the following people:*

Ed, Joanne, Rachel and Felice Steele for being an extended family who fed me many good dinners and distracted me from work when I needed a break.

Kim Solga and Jane Seeley for excellent, precise proofreading, though any remaining errors are my responsibility.

Alan Cornwell and Peter Dale, my printers, along with their staff at Ram Offset, for encouraging me and teaching me about pre-press and printing work.

Tim Larive and Dorian Aiello for advice and moral support when I was deciding to publish the book myself.

*And Jenny thanks these people:*

My husband, Michael Zanger, and my stepkids, Chris and Sierra, for their love, support, and humor.

My mentors, Jim Mayer, Jim Hayes, and Marge Apperson, for years of journalistic encouragement.

David Burson for helping my computer talk to Jane's.

*Finally, we both thank:*

The photographers and writers who made this book possible.

Mount Shasta City          Kevin Lahey →

# Shasta Grace Gibson

*Shasta Grace Gibson's mother had only seen photos of Mt. Shasta when she and her husband decided to give their new baby daughter the mountain's name. Audra Gibson explained that her husband Mark had climbed the mountain, and while she had been near it twice, clouds kept her from viewing it.*

*"Shasta was born in Oakland on February 18, 1989," Audra said. "We were in awe of the mountain, and giving our daughter its name was a way we could honor her."*

*The Gibsons own a stock photo business called Gibson Color Photography, and were living in Richmond when their daughter was born. They moved to the community of Mount Shasta in 1992.*

*"We put out there the possibility of a move, and the next thing we knew, we were pulled in. We'd given ourselves three years to get here, but a year and a half later we were living in the house we live in now," Audra said.*

*Audra made her first ascent of Mount Shasta in 1993. Known as "Audrey" all her life, she signed "Audra" in the summit register and has preferred that name ever since.*

Shasta Lily                                    Bob Gray

*The following is an interview with 6–year–old Shasta Grace Gibson.*

Q: Is it good or bad to have the same name as a mountain?

A: It's good. Because when you hear people, and they're talking about the mountain, you can turn around and say, "What?" if you hear them say "Shasta." It's fun to turn around and say, "What?" like they were talking about you.

Q: What do people say when you tell them your name is Shasta?

A: They say it's a nice name, or "I like it."

Q: What do you like about the mountain?

A: The snow never melts. It's pretty.

Q: What do you like to do on the mountain?

A: Feed the nutcrackers (birds) up at Horse Camp and go sledding at Bunny Flat. I fly really high above the ground.

Q: Do you have any stories from when you were on Mount Shasta?

A: Once I hiked up to Horse Camp with my daddy and he put some bread on his nose and a bird came down and ate it off his nose.

Q: Do you want to climb Mount Shasta someday?

A: Maybe. I don't know.

Q: How old should you be to climb it?

A: At least 21, because my legs might get a little tired if I'm any younger than that.

Q: What would you see on top?

A: Lots of rocks, and a little tiny book on the top. I have a book that looks just like it.

Q: What would you write in the book at the top?

A: I might change my name.

Q: What would you change it to?

A: (After thinking awhile...) To Abbie.

Q: Why Abbie?

A: Because I think it's a pretty name.

Q: When do you like the mountain the best?

A: I like it with snow on it and with a rainbow over the top as a hat.

Rowena Pattee Kryder

# Jan Driessen

*Jan Driessen learned to fly a sailplane, or glider, when he was an 18-year-old in Holland, his home country. His family lived next to an air base, and all of the aviation activity intrigued him.*

*When Jan felt he was ready to learn to fly, there were no private, powered airplanes available; this was Holland in 1954, the post-war years. That's why he tried his wings in a glider, and he's been flying one ever since.*

*He moved to Siskiyou County in 1971 when he went to work for Bank of America's Yreka branch. Jan retired as vice president/manager of the branch after 34 years with the company.*

*He found Siskiyou County to be an excellent place to soar. In fact, Jan is what is called a Diamond Pilot, which is like being a black belt in karate. He has kept his glider in the sky for six hours at a time.*

*Jan, now a gliding instructor, related the following experience.*

Several years ago I flew out of Tulelake, on Mount Shasta's northeast side, in my beautiful glider, a Libelle, which means "dragonfly" in German. It was an excellent soaring day so the glider and I climbed out over Captain Jack's Stronghold, flew over Lava Beds National Monument, and headed for Medicine Lake.

Glider                                                            Michael Zanger

While climbing I watched Mount Shasta in the distance. Or was Shasta watching me? The cumulus clouds covered the 12,000 foot level and up. I had never been close to Shasta. But this time some unexplained force beckoned me from about 40 miles away: "Come over here, little dragonfly. Come visit!"

I flew the Libelle closer and closer to the mountain. The massive rock and snow touched the clouds and from where I was, it looked like the earth stopped there. The closer I soared, the more and more massive Mount Shasta became.

Whaleback Mountain passed by me on the right, and lift was so strong that I could soar straight without turning and without losing altitude. Was Mount Shasta helping me to visit her?

I now approached the snow line of her north side—steep, very steep, massive, and overwhelming. I slowed the Libelle down and cruised by the 12,000 foot level, right underneath the clouds. It was as if I was soaring underneath the awning of a huge patio.

It was very quiet, and I saw no one. Yet, I felt as if somebody (or something) was watching me. Words that come to mind to explain that experience would be "awesome," "overpowering," "eerie," and "fantastic."

I made a turn next to the rim of Shastina, and quietly flew back next to the crater and over the Whitney Glacier toward Tulelake.

What a flight! What a visit! Thank you, Mount Shasta, for inviting me to that incredible visit. Oh yes, I will never forget, and I will always respect you.

Shastina                                              Jane English

Anthony Colburn →

# Missi Gillespie

Late on a summer's day in August, 1973 I drove south from Oregon, winding through the mountains of Siskiyou County for the first time. A sweeping curve suddenly turned the road out onto a plain; the landscape glowed with pastel shades of purple, pinks and blues. Suspended in the distant mist was the tracing of a beautiful snow–capped mountain.

My eyes filled with tears. My heart felt like it melted. I knew this was my spiritual home, Shangri–La...Mount Shasta.

After my first glimpse, I went to the mountain as often as possible. There were times when I was called in the middle of the night to leave immediately and drive to the mountain. I always went, sensing from the beginning its commanding presence and energy.

One day, after walking and meditating on the mountain, I returned to my car, at the end of the paved road coming up from town. Just as I began my descent, a voice clearly said, "This is Home. Come and live here." Startled, I stopped the car and looked around. I was alone, yet immediately responded to the voice: "I will move here. It will take awhile to reorganize my life."

Heading down, I reflected on what had just happened and was struck by the absolute clarity of the interaction. I was staying with my friend Dorothy Kingsland, who owned the Golden Bough Bookstore in town, a spiritual resource place for the community. Over the years I had slept on the bookstore floor or couch and watched other pilgrims come through the store on their way to and from the mountain. Person after person would come in and share wondrous stories of meetings and events that had a magically transformative quality for their lives. People were coming from all over the world to pay homage to this sacred site and to place their prayers. Now I, too, had been touched by its power.

Six years after the parking lot experience, I had finally unwired a complex life and deepened my commitment to spirit. It soon became obvious to Dorothy and me that now was the time I should move here and take over the store from her.

Heart Lake      Michael Zanger

That was nine years ago. Since then this bookstore has been full of warmth, joy, tears, and the love of thousands who, aware of it or not, are connected to the mountain. Some visit; others find a way to remain here.

Just a few moments ago a woman named Judith walked into the store and said, "I thought I knew what 'sacred' meant. I just came down from the mountain. I didn't really know before, and just got a glimpse of real sacredness. I got a vision of starting a business at this mountain. I'm coming!"

People come here attracted to the lore of the mountain. Stories abound about another civilization beneath Shasta's craggy surface, a race of tall people — Lemurians, they're called — who leave their cities through hidden entrances and come to town to trade with gold nuggets. Spaceship sightings are another set of stories; I admit to seeing one, as do many people here from all walks of life.

Whether by word of mouth, radio and television programs, airline travelogues, or simply an inner voice, people are drawn here. For some, just hearing the name or seeing an image of the mountain is enough.

Early one morning a woman called me from Kentucky. She had fallen asleep in front of her television and woke with a start just as a picture of Mount Shasta came onto the screen. She watched the show, in which I was interviewed, and by the time it was over she felt compelled to come to Mount Shasta immediately. She was calling me just so that someone would know that something powerful was happening to her. During the next week she held yard sales and sold everything. Exactly seven days after the call, she appeared in the store, suitcases in hand, a happy new resident.

A middle–aged man excitedly pointed to the store's guest book one day. "Tell me, please, this woman who last signed — did you see her? Where did she go?" I told him that she had been directed to a nearby restaurant for lunch. He rushed from the store, and returned an hour later, hand in hand with his long–lost love. She had come to the mountain to pray for her life's companion. They later sent me a wedding invitation.

A man comes in once a month from Los Angeles; a couple from San Francisco come here every weekend. Others make the journey each summer, all for nourishment of the spirit.

People feel called and compelled to be here at the mountain. Not a few, but thousands. They come to attend concerts, to take or lead workshops, to chant, to pray, or to simply "Be." The veil of spiritual dimensions is thin on this one of seven sacred mountains of the world. Here, for so many, heaven and earth meet.

We are so Blessed.

Jane English

15

# Frank Seywald

*Frank Seywald is among those who have loved Mount Shasta for a lifetime, but do not live within the mountain's view. While that arrangement creates its own frustrations, the beauty is that, for Frank, Mount Shasta has become "a serene place in the mind."*

*Frank describes himself as a "city boy" who grew up in San Francisco and became interested in technical and mechanical trades as the result of childhood hobbies, such as building model airplanes. He apprenticed as a machinist in a shipyard and later worked as a tool and die maker, while at the same time taking night school classes in liberal arts, business, and engineering.*

*For 20 years he held management positions in the aerospace industry. Then, after getting involved with a small community theater group in Jackson, California, he bought a motel there and moved to the country. He sold the motel in 1993 after owning it for 25 years.*

*Frank, now age 71, used to visit Mount Shasta two or three times a year. His journeys to the mountain's slopes are now annual, but the photographs and paintings of Mount Shasta that adorn his den ensure constant thoughts of the mountain.*

*"If I don't think about it every day, then I think about it at night," Frank says. "You know how you wake up at 3 a.m. and think about your career, places you've hiked, people you've met. As I get older, and get closer to that 'big crevasse,' I'm more keenly aware of those precious memories."*

*Frank wrote the following.*

As a San Francisco teenager over five decades ago, by lucky chance I was seduced by the Goddess Shasta. It happened when my beloved older brother, Vernon Howard, needed a compliant flunky to help get his cranky old Willys coupe to Oregon so that he could climb with friends.

He gave me no warning of the majestic white beacon that evolved from the clouds as we drove up the Sacramento Valley. The first views presented immense contrast to the city streets and local hills that I had walked many a mile, exploring what was available. Never had I seen such a dominant mass, yet so beautiful, demure, and serene. I was smitten and I vowed to be back to walk up this lovely 'higher hill' that looked so easy to my novice eyes.

Vern was a mountaineering book dealer, so I was soon immersed in reading everything available about Mount Shasta history and keen to begin the first of many pilgrimages to this unique siren of nature. We started in the early 1940's with just Vern and I together, and then went on to spread the Mount Shasta gospel to many dozens of urban friends. With various small groups, we learned elementary climbing methods by trial and error. The free spirit of the mountain gave a refreshing respite from our city roots.

In those times, high–tech equipment was boots with hob–nails and a heavy homemade ice–ax or an alpenstock. Also, the budget limits meant weighty army surplus skis, tents, and backpacks. Transportation from the Bay Area was often via hitchhiking or the Greyhound bus, which passed through the town of Mount Shasta at about 3 a.m. In the dark we packed our gear,

From Lake Siskiyou

Jane English

loaded with canned food, and hiked to McBride Springs for our Camp 1, to share space with nosy porcupines.

The next step to Horse Camp had some random old signs lying along the trail that stated the mileage from 'Sisson,' obviously left from earlier times before the town's name changed. It's hard to believe today, but one June then, Vern, our sister Betsy and I trudged through the snow and spent a whole week there without seeing another person.

Usually we had the pleasure of meeting very few, but always gifted people, such as mountaineer and Horse Camp caretaker Ed Stuhl, or botanist William Bridge Cook, who typically would stay for days before climbing to the summit, or to Shastina, or around the mountain at timberline. Warm, intellectual debates were a campsite ritual and memorable friendships were formed, with the common bond of the spirit of Shasta. Many of that era have since ascended to ethereal summits, but they will always be part of the enhancement of the mountain. Shasta symbolizes nature's excelsior and it also reflects the special people who are part of its uniqueness. My frequent thoughts of love for the mountain are intertwined with fond memories of Shasta's people.

Now, in concert with the global population expansion, the mountain shares the planet's problems. My experiences of 50 years ago are no longer available in these times, just as I wasn't able to exactly duplicate the days of John Muir, Clarence King, and Justin Sisson. However, even infrequent visits today are still most rewarding.

We must do our utmost to maintain this psychic oasis for our heirs. As one positive step for the next generation, I'm fabricating alpenstocks for our grandchildren.

Climbers in Avalanche Gulch          Anthony Colburn  →

Many come to the mountain on spiritual journeys: Christians, Buddhists, Jews, channelers, new age seekers, shamans, and others of many different practices. The spirit of the mountain knows no religion and accepts all without prejudice.

— *Jennifer Hall*

Tibetan Monk                    Michael Zanger

Many thousands of people from all walks of life and different religions feel a special love for Mount Shasta as a spiritual sanctuary unique in North America, just as people the world over honor Mount Fuji in Japan, Mount Kilimanjaro in Tanzania and the lofty peaks of the Himalayas.

— *Michelle Berditchevsky*

Anthony Colburn

This mountain is considered to be one of the seven sacred mountains of the world. Spiritual leaders from many lineages come here on pilgrimage. For many thousands of us, in our hearts this place is home.

— *Missi Gillespie*

Alpenglow    Michael Zanger →

# Donna Brooks

Except for the year she attended beauty college in Santa Rosa, Donna Kohn Brooks has lived each of her 78 years in Mount Shasta. The stories of her ancestors, and of her own childhood, reflect the history of the town that was first named Berryvale, then Sisson, and finally Mount Shasta.

Donna's grandparents on her father's side, Nicholas and Katherine Kohn, moved from the country of Luxembourg to the Arbuckle, California area, and then to Sisson in 1888. Katherine had malaria, and the couple heard that there was good, healing water in Sisson.

Nicholas was hired by the railroad, but two years later moved to Ash Creek where he worked in the mill. In late 1899 they bought the Mountain House, a way station where ranchers would rest when they herded their cattle from the Fall River Valley to be put on the train in Sisson.

A hunting accident took Nicholas' life in 1900 and Katherine was left alone to rear five children. She continued to operate the Mountain House, and raised vegetables to be sold in McCloud. In 1903 she moved her family to Sisson, built a house on Chestnut Street, and opened a livery stable. In 1910 she built the Ramshaw Building on the corner of Castle Street and Mount Shasta Boulevard, which currently houses Ace Hardware. Sisson is where Donna's father, also named Nicholas, and his siblings spent most of their childhood. In his teen years, Nicholas worked as a guide on Mount Shasta.

On the maternal side, Donna's mother Flossie was born to Mary and John Morrison in Missouri in 1899. Mary Morrison died of tuberculosis in 1906. Three years later, John married Cora Cotton, and the family moved from Missouri to Sisson in 1914. One of John's first jobs in town was lighting the gas street lights on the main street. He also cut ice at Abrams Lake and worked at the state fish hatchery and as a seasonal employee for the U.S. Forest Service.

Flossie Morrison and Nicholas Kohn met and were married in 1916. Flossie was 17 years old, and Nicholas was 26. Nicholas was a self–employed plumber and concrete worker who eventually hired on to the city's public works crew.

Donna was born in 1917 in the very house where her mother still lives on Alder and Ivy Streets in Mount Shasta. Her brother Leonard "Bud" Kohn was also born there, in 1918. Donna attended Mount Shasta schools, and in 1945 married Ralph Brooks. The couple had a daughter, Dawn, who in turn had three children: Bryan, Mindy, and Timothy. Mindy now has a daughter, Sierra, which means that there are currently five generations living on the Kohn–Morrison side of the family. Ralph and Donna were divorced in 1974.

Long–time Mount Shasta residents and visitors alike remember the popular Windsor's Drugstore, famous for its homemade ice cream, Emery Wheels, and thick milkshakes. The store, which closed in 1989, is also part of Donna's personal history. Her brother Bud started working as a pharmacist at Windsor's in 1940, upon his graduation from the University of California. Bud bought out one partner in 1945, and Ralph and Donna bought out the other partner in 1949. Ralph sold his half of the store to Bud in 1979, and 10 years later Bud retired. The store was sold to Payless Drugs, bringing an end to independent drugstores in the area.

Donna is interested in her personal family history, and over the years she has also documented the history of the town and its inhabitants, writing numerous pieces for the Siskiyou Pioneer, the yearbook of the Siskiyou County Historical Society. She edited the 1981 issue on Mount Shasta. She also compiled a book on the 100–year history of the Methodist Church in Mount Shasta.

She was co–chairperson of the Mount Shasta Centennial in 1987; has been active with the Mount Shasta Community Concert Association,

Jane English

Sisson Museum, county elections board, and the Know Your Heirlooms group; and in 1987 was named Mount Shasta Citizen of the Year.

As for growing up with Mount Shasta in her backyard, Donna says she remembers hiking to Horse Camp and partway up Olberman's Causeway in the 1930's. She also has fond memories of working with the Mount Shasta Herald Ski School at the Mount Shasta Ski Bowl for 10 years.

But she never felt compelled to climb to the top of the mountain.

"I just never thought of it," she says. "I'm lazy, I guess. I thought I was pretty lucky to get up to Horse Camp."

"I look at the mountain every day, though. If you stand at the kitchen sink in Mom's house, you look right out at the mountain. When we built on to our house, we put this window right where you could look at the mountain. When the power company put in poles, I had to have them change the location of one so it wouldn't block our view."

"I think the mountain must have some kind of power to attract people, but maybe that's just its beauty. I don't believe in UFOs or Lemurians. I do like to watch the cloud formations that go around the mountain. I don't 'read' them like some people do, but lots of times you can pick out animals and other shapes."

"You can always see something different in the mountain: the shadows, or the clouds, or the color of it. The sunsets are so beautiful. When there's an especially pink one we call the mountain a 'strawberry ice cream cone.'"

"I remember one day, when I stopped at the supermarket to pick something up on my way home from the museum, I saw a woman standing in the street taking a picture. I turned around and saw that the mountain was covered perfectly with this white cap. It was like a perfect dome–shaped cloud completely hiding the mountain. I'd never seen anything like that before."

"As for the mountain being a volcano, I don't worry about it. I just think about it as a mountain, not as a volcano. And even if it does blow one day, I don't imagine I'll be around to see it."

Jane English

# Cheryl Yambrach Rose

*Mount Shasta visionary artist Cheryl Yambrach Rose first expressed herself on canvas with Western–style scenes, and once traded paintings for two Arabian horses. Her work from that era has been featured in the book* Contemporary Western Artists, *and has been shown at the Nelson Rockefeller Collection and in many museums.*

"*Those were productive years, yet I felt an emptiness inside, like I should be doing something else,*" *Cheryl says.* "*The transformation to visionary art occurred during my reception at the Rockefeller Collection. It was every artist's dream of a reception: caviar, furs, and glitz.*"

*The owner of the Rockefeller Collection appreciated her Western art, but told her that no visionary art would be accepted. Cheryl made the decision to return home and paint only her visions from the heart.*

*Each image is designed, she says, "to impart a feeling of alignment and harmony, and to reveal the radiance of one's being through the 'keys' and archetypes of the visionary process." Cheryl paints in "parables," images that connote a great range of meaning and may be understood directly by the subconscious as well as the conscious mind.*

*Her studio was built according to sacred geometry on the ancient Celtic foundation pattern of Glastonbury Abbey and Stonehenge, centered around the number 12.*

Jane English

*Over the past 18 years she has worked to build a spiritual bridge between Mount Shasta and sacred sites in England. Most recently she created 17 paintings to illustrate the book* Mythical Journeys and Legendary Quests, *by British writer Moyra Caldecott. Also, Cheryl is one of several guides on a travel tour in England called "The Quest for King Arthur's Avalon."*

I lived on the north side of Mount Shasta for 10 years, mainly working on my Western art. It was five years before I even tried to paint the mountain, and then it was another five years before I actually learned how to paint it. It's not an easy thing to paint.

In 1976 I started making fairly regular trips to Glastonbury, England, but it was not until 1990 that I gained an awareness that Glastonbury and Mount Shasta should share a connection as power places. I realized it wasn't an accident that I kept going back and forth between them. I've worked hard to build a bridge between the two. In Glastonbury there are four stores where you can find cards and posters with Mount Shasta in them. In Cornwall and Tintagel they love the image of Mount Shasta, too. I've tried to establish the mountain as a holy place in the world, because it is.

I've learned from building this bridge that Mount Shasta and Glastonbury can benefit from each other. I refer to Glastonbury as "the heart," and Mount Shasta as "the crown." In England I feel a gentle energy. We need more of the greenness, groundedness, and heart–place of England. Mount Shasta is more in the angelic realms, the higher spiritual realms. There's a lot of historical vibration in England, but in Mount Shasta the vibration is pretty pure, fresh and new, and it's that energy which I try to bring back to England.

Mount Shasta is like a clearing ground, constantly bombarding you with challenges. Another door opens and you get through that one, then another one opens. It's a constant process here. It motivates you to feel and do the ultimate of what you're capable of doing; there's a sense of urgency here.

The mountain is about infusing spirit into matter, and that's what my work is about. This is a place where these things can be brought forth easily. My Second Sight, which I inherited from the Cornish ancestry on my mother's side, is really developed here. There's not a lot of interference in the air. Instead, there is clarity. I think that's what we have here.

The mountain, for me, is a living archetype. Its message is that it's time to get going; it's time to get serious. When I've been away and I'm riding up Interstate 5 and see it on the horizon, my back gets straight and I realize it's time to go back to work—back to my painting as well as my spiritual work. To me this isn't a place to play. I feel like we're here to work, to do our life's purpose. Everyone has something to offer.

Jane English

# William Hirt

*Imagine the ancient geologic tales that lie in the ridges, rocks, and valleys of the volcano named Mount Shasta. It must truly be a geologist's heaven.*

*Dr. William Hirt is familiar with those tales. Currently a geology instructor at College of the Siskiyous, he holds a Master of Science degree from the University of California at Los Angeles, and a Ph.D. from the University of California at Santa Barbara.*

*Before moving to the Mount Shasta area he taught at the University of Arizona and University of North Carolina, and worked on a regional mapping project for the Idaho Geological Survey.*

*He wrote the following explanation of Mount Shasta's history, drawing on studies conducted by former College of the Siskiyous geologist Paul Dawson, and U.S. Geological Survey geologists Dan Miller and Bob Christianson.*

As you drive along Interstate 5 through Siskiyou County in Northern California, mountains flank you on either side.

To the west stand the Klamath Mountains, which consist of blocks of ocean floor crust and sediment that have been folded and faulted into their present positions. To the east stands Mount Shasta and several lesser peaks of the Cascade Range that have been built by flows of lava and ash. As different as these two ranges are, both are the result of the same geologic process: subduction.

The North American continent is part of a large plate of the Earth's crust that is moving slowly southwestward over the deeper mantle. Along the Pacific Northwest coast, from Cape Mendocino to southern British Columbia, North America is overriding several smaller plates of oceanic crust. As these plates are pushed down into the mantle—or subducted— sediment and pieces of ocean crust are scraped off and added on to the leading edge of the continent, forming the Klamaths.

The downgoing plates also carry seawater into the mantle. As the plates are heated, this water is released and causes the surrounding rocks to melt. These partially melted rocks, called magmas, then rise buoyantly through the crust. Some erupt to form Cascade volcanoes, while others cool slowly and solidify at depth to form bodies of crystalline rock called plutons. Such bodies may later be exposed by erosion, as the Castle Crags pluton has been.

Subduction has continued along the Northwest coast for many millions of years, but the young Cascade peaks that we see today record only a short span of this activity.

The Mount Shasta volcanic center, for example, has been active for about 600,000 years. A large mountain called ancestral Mount Shasta once stood on the site of today's peak. About 350,000 years ago the north flank of this volcano collapsed, forming a great landslide that swept out across the Shasta Valley. The small hills that lie just east of Interstate 5 between Weed and Yreka are blocks of the old mountain that were carried in the slide.

No one knows what caused ancestral Mount Shasta to collapse, but we do know that as volcanoes age, they become more susceptible to slope failure. Magma rising into a volcanic cone circulates hot, sulfurous ground water that alters fresh lavas and ash to clay. This clay is much weaker than the original rocks and, over time, a volcano will become "rotten" inside. Once Mount Shasta's predecessor

Mount Shasta from the Klamath Mountains                    Shari Nordell

had been altered, the shaking of an earthquake or the added weight of water from a wet winter might have been enough to trigger the slide.

The present Mount Shasta has been built during the past 250,000 years in a series of four eruptive episodes. The first episode formed the Sargent's Ridge cone, whose glaciated core rises above the Old Ski Bowl. Subsequent eruptions added Misery Hill, Shastina and, finally, the Hotlum dome, which forms the present summit.

Each episode began with violent eruptions from a central vent that sent hot flows of rock and gas sweeping down the mountain's flanks. Weed and Mount Shasta City are both built on deposits from such flows that occurred about 9,400 years ago during the Shastina eruptive episode. As each episode drew to a close, a plug of pasty lava welled up into the vent, sealing it and building a rounded dome. Black Butte is such a dome, although it formed low on the flank of the mountain rather than at one of its major eruptive centers.

Today Mount Shasta is relatively quiet, as it has been during much of its history. Each of the eruptive episodes that contributed to the mountain's growth is thought to have lasted only a few hundred to a few thousand years. Between these periods of activity, glaciers have carved into the peak and mudflows have coursed down the creeks that drain its flanks. At present, in fact, mudflows caused by heavy rains or an abnormally warm spring may be one of the greatest threats the mountain poses to nearby communities.

As long as subduction continues along the Pacific Northwest coast, so will the threat of eruptions from Mount Shasta and other Cascade volcanoes. Studies of the mountain's past activity suggest that residents of Siskiyou County have about a one in three or four chance of witnessing an eruption during their lifetimes.

The magmas that feed these eruptions seldom rise to the surface without making their presence known well in advance, however. The occurrence of shallow earthquakes, bulging of the ground surface, and increases in the temperatures of thermal springs may all herald the onset of a volcanic eruption.

Mount Shasta is being monitored for seismic activity and swelling by members of the U.S. Geological Survey in an effort to predict the timing and location of any future eruptions, and so minimize injuries or damage they might cause.

Mark Gibson →

# Bob Gray

*In 1942, Bob Gray hitchhiked from his home state of Louisiana to Mount Shasta to take a job with the U.S. Forest Service. During his 35 years with the agency, Bob worked 20 years as a fire control officer overseeing Fall River Mills, then Weaverville, and finally Mount Shasta from 1960 to 1977. He also worked stints as a fire lookout, snow surveyor, dispatcher, phone line repairman, fire crew foreman, seed cone collector, road surveyor, sandblaster, rescue worker, pack animal handler — and even more. His experiences, from humorous to dramatic, are written in the book* Forests, Fires, and Wild Things, *which was published in 1985. Bob, now age 73, lives in a log cabin in McCloud with his wife, Betty.*

Generally speaking, fires on Mount Shasta are different from others in the area. You don't tend to get big ones because the fires at higher elevations are easier to put out. They're usually not spectacular, either. The fires with the most potential are in the lower elevations.

Fires on the north don't burn as hot as they do on the south side because the north side is cooler, the humidity is higher, and you don't get the winds. The south side gets sun so the temperatures are higher, the humidity is lower, and the winds are higher. That's where the big ones can happen.

One fire really intrigued me, on the side of Shasta, fairly high up. I dispatched a crew, got a line around the fire, and suddenly, this huge cumulus cloud came and created wildly erratic winds. The fire exploded in all directions. It burned 500 to 600 acres. That can happen with a huge cumulus cloud because in the mature stage of a cumulus, air spills straight down and literally fans the fire.

We recruited men to fight fires from all sorts of places. Sawmills and logging operations were the best source, but hunters and the man on the street would do. Many millworkers and woodworkers enjoyed the diversity of being on the fireline, though not all shared this enjoyment.

One weekend the local mill wasn't running, so we were unable to get a crew from them. Dutch decided we'd better recruit from the street and from the McCloud Hotel, where most of the bachelor workers lived. We had signed up a few men, but the word must have gone faster than we had. When we knocked on one door in the hotel a voice answered, "I'm sick in bed."

Dutch opened the door, and sure enough, the man was in bed. I was totally shocked when Dutch took hold of the covers and yanked them off. The sick man was fully clothed, including boots. It seems Dutch knew this fellow and told him, "You fooled me last time, but you can't fool me twice." The "sick" logger grinned and reported to the Forest Service as requested.

In the 1960's we were doing a lot of "type conversion," where we converted brush acreage to a tree plantation. We'd use bulldozers to clear around the perimeter of the area to be burned. Then we'd crush it and let it stand for a season. On the chosen burn day we'd use a drip torch that dribbles diesel and gas to light the fire.

There are certain guidelines you follow. For instance, you don't burn if the wind is over five miles per hour, or if the humidity is less than 20%.

There is always a calculated risk in using fire as a tool in forestry, and I've had two serious mishaps, both in 1967. It was a bad year for me. I'll tell you first about the "Oops Fire."

It was a beautiful mid–May morning. Conditions were borderline, in that we were crowding our burning guidelines all the way. Even so, I decided that with all our expertise and plans, the worst that could happen would be a few spot fires which we could pick up without too much trouble. After all, the snow had not been off the adjacent brush very long, and there were still a few snowbanks on the shady side of the trees on the uphill side of the burn. We were situated on the lower flanks of the mountain as you see it from the town of Mount Shasta.

Underestimating the potential intensity and rate of spread, I unwisely started firing the wrong end of the area, figuring we would need the extra heat to insure a clean burn.

Now, Tom, who was working with me, was not a very scientific fire behavior specialist, but he did know that fires burn uphill faster than downhill, and that a tail wind is going to spread it faster, still.

"Bob," he said to me that day, "do you know that this fire is going right across the line and up that draw if we light it the way you want us to?"

Smokey Sunrise                                                                                            Jane English

"Aw, Tom, you're a pessimist," I said. "We can hold it with the tankers and Don's dozer."

Tom was right on all counts. Within an hour we were in bad trouble. The fire didn't just spot across the line—it roared across, and headed up the draw with the fury of a tornado.

I was right about one thing. It burned clean, both inside and outside the planned area.

We managed to hold the north end at the Everitt Memorial Highway by picking up a few spots across the highway, but not before burning about 20 acres of private land and several acres of Forest Service plantation adjacent to the area. It also burned a few scattered trees in a brush patch not within the planned burn. We'd planned to burn 160 acres, but a total of nearly 300 extra acres were consumed by the escaped fire, which finally stopped at the snowbanks in the timber above the brush.

I could really not blame anyone but myself for the escaped fire. Lee, the ranger who named the fire, was very understanding, and graciously accepted part of the responsibility. Tom still has never said, "I told you so."

Then there was the "Shasta Escape" that same year. We had planned a 1,000 acre burn, but when it got away from us it burned about 1,300 extra acres, most of which was Southern Pacific land. You can still look up and see the lines of the "Shasta Escape."

Still, my friends said that was the spot for the greatest buck hunting that year. They'd never seen better.

Snow Surveyor - 1940's

Ted Graves

Bass Lake - Shasta Valley                                              John Jackson

Lake Shastina Resort   Kevin Lahey

Lake Siskiyou          Mark Gibson

If bread is the first necessity of life, recreation is a close second.
— *Edward Bellamy 1850-1898*

South of Weed                                    John Jackson

Hot Air Balloons in Shasta Valley                          Kevin Lahey

Jane English →

# Kristen Meyer

*Thousands of people visit Mount Shasta every year, and Kristen Meyer is one of the people who want to make sure those visitors enjoy the mountain without harming it. Kristen has a bachelor's degree in Environmental Studies and a master's degree in Recreation Administration.*

*After working for the National Park Service in Yosemite, Mount Rainier, and Alaska, she was hired in 1989 by the U.S. Forest Service as a wilderness ranger on Mount Shasta.*

*Kristen was interviewed in the midst of a busy summer season.*

**Q.** What kinds of people have you met as a wilderness ranger on Mount Shasta?

**A.** People from all walks of life, all ages, all nationalities:

Lots of local people enjoying their back yard. Native Americans who regard it as a church where the creator lives. People looking for Lemurians and tunnels in the mountain. People in search of a spiritual awakening or their own enlightenment. Families from other states who get out of the car at the end of the road, look around, climb back in the car, and drive off.

City dwellers looking for a break from the structure of their busy lives. People doing naked yoga in the parking lot at the Old Ski Bowl. Climbers wondering what it's like up there, or training for bigger climbs. People who describe paranormal visions or see UFOs. Drummers and chanters, especially during the full moon in August. Local skiers enjoying the mountain for the day.

People who remember the Old Ski Bowl and come to see what the area looks like now.

Europeans taking a look at America's mountains. A Korean girl seeing snow for the first time, making snowballs. Locals taking their friends or relatives for a drive up the mountain. Deer hunters and bird watchers. Geology and botany enthusiasts.

Mount Shasta's following is vast and diverse. Nothing surprises me anymore.

**Q.** What kinds of problems do people create when they use the mountain?

**A.** Impacts result any time lots of people visit a popular area. The difficult question is which impacts are considered acceptable, and how can impacts be managed to preserve the area. Some impacts, like noise or litter, are short-term and easily corrected. Unfortunately, other impacts are not as easy to repair.

When I arrived in 1989, I found garbage and graffiti in Panther and Squaw meadows, and felt an alarming sense of damage from over-use. There were few well-marked trails and little effort being made to educate people about how to care for this fragile alpine environment. The mountain was not being stewarded in a way that would preserve its special qualities over time. I decided that meadow damage and human waste were the biggest use issues.

Meadows became the priority because of the potential for long-term, irreversible effects. Since then the meadows have become a real success story. With assistance from the University of California at Berkeley we conducted a survey of plant communities in the meadows, and mapped existing trails, which were just a random network created by users. We figured out which trails were the most efficient and appropriate and kept them open and signed them. We closed the other trails and rehabilitated them by allowing natural regeneration of vegetation, supplemented with plants grown in the Forest Service greenhouse. We also eliminated camping and campfires in the meadows and started making regular on-site visits to work personally with people.

Most people were not doing anything maliciously; they were just ignorant about the cumulative impacts. We have seen a vast improvement. In a sense we've stopped the bleeding. It's not getting worse, but it will take a long time for those areas to regenerate.

Then there is the human waste problem, which exists mainly in the Avalanche Gulch climbing route, and particularly at Lake Helen, where many climbers spend the night. We studied what others do, and decided to adopt a system similar to those of Yosemite, Mount Rainier, and Mount Hood. We're benefiting from experiments in other areas.

We now issue "waste kits" with a Ziploc bag containing two paper bags with a handful of kitty litter in them. People carry their waste with them, and at Bunny Flat, deposit the paper bags in the vault toilets, and the Ziploc

Panther Meadow                    Jane English

bags in the garbage. Monitoring will tell us if this system works. We'll keep trying until we find a long-term solution.

**Q.** What's your advice to people using the mountain?

**A.** My hope is that visitors will know and care enough to do what is best for whatever ecosystem they happen to be in. A land ethic or deep caring for the land comes from within; it cannot be mandated or legislated. Good decision-making based on accurate information and a solid land ethic will help preserve our wildlands for future generations.

Most mountain etiquette is based on common sense that applies anywhere, like pack out what you pack in, leave plants and rocks where they are, and use established trails, campsites and fire rings. There are a few things specific to the Mount Shasta Wilderness: bring a stove as wood fires are not allowed, leave pets at home, and travel in groups of 10 or fewer. Being knowledgeable and prepared allows for deeper enjoyment of the mountain's splendor.

**Q.** What are your personal feelings about the mountain?

**A.** I have learned so much from the mountain. Every person I've met has shown me a different meaning or perspective on what Mount Shasta is. My personal philosophy has been to listen carefully to the range of experiences, from the far-out to the very mundane.

I appreciate that the mountain is a teacher for people, and lets us see our smallness, and what it means to move toward a more unified community. To stay polarized is to fail to understand the lesson it teaches us. The mountain transcends petty viewpoints.

My favorite time is when I'm out alone on a more remote part of the mountain, just experiencing it first-hand. Or being on the other side of the valley floor and looking back at it. I like finding a place to be quiet enough to really listen with a different level of attention. That's when I find myself closest to what the mountain means to me. It's hard to put into words, but I always carry it with me.

George Stroud →

# Frank Christina

*Weather has fascinated Frank Christina for as long as he can remember. He has kept weather records since he was a young teenager growing up in Los Angeles — a boring place to live if the weather is your thing, he says.*

*But mountain weather is Frank's passion. He and his wife Ann moved to Mount Shasta in 1972 and Frank started keeping unofficial weather records, often comparing them with official records kept at that time by National Weather Service meteorologist Wade English. When Wade passed away in 1985, Frank replaced him as the area's official observer.*

*Every day Frank is responsible for recording the high temperature, low temperature, and precipitation, including snowfall, for the past 24–hour period. The finely–calibrated equipment is located in his backyard in the city of Mount Shasta, so the statistics may differ from what is happening, weather–wise, on the mountain itself.*

*With Ann's help, Frank managed to keep records during his recent kidney transplant. A sawmill worker by trade, Frank's duty as a weather observer is a volunteer labor of love.*

The most outstanding change of weather I've ever experienced was here in Mount Shasta. It was July 1987 and it started with a good–sized thunderstorm that dropped 1.5 inches of rain in 45 minutes. Then, later the same month, we had a high of 102 degrees, which broke a record for that date. Finally, three days later, we had a high of 47 degrees in a 24–hour period, and snow fell to 5,000 feet on Mount Shasta. It was incredible!

The record high in the city of Mount Shasta was 105 degrees in August of 1981, and the record low was –13 degrees in December of 1990. There are lots of great records. For instance, the average snowfall here in a year is 96 inches. The record for snowfall in town in one season was 270.5 inches during the winter of 1889–90. The winter of 1936–37 was also a doozy with 236 inches of snow.

But then, the winter of 1936–37 was a very cold winter everywhere; it even snowed in Sacramento and Chico. During the month of January 1937 there was only one day where the temperature got above freezing in Mount Shasta. The normal for January is four days of 32 degrees or less. That month blew all the records to heck.

The record for the most snowfall in one 24–hour period was set on a day in December 1952 when 37 inches fell. That's a lot of snow in one day.

Records for rainfall were set very recently. We got 27.48 inches of rain in January 1995, which is the highest ever for any single month. Then March of 1995 set a record for the most rainfall in March—18.86 inches.

Storms have always fascinated me. I like the energy that's produced, the wind, the sound of thunder. I don't think there's a better sound on earth, especially a late summer thunderstorm when you hear a clap of thunder in the distance.

When I was in the hospital in Portland getting my kidney transplant, they had the curtains closed so I couldn't see out the window. I told my wife, "Open the drapes! I've got to see what's happening with the weather! It's a free show—compliments of Mother Nature."

Los Angeles is a lousy place to live if you watch weather, and although I'm intrigued by mountain weather, I'd say it was Mount Shasta itself that made us move here. We were planning to move to Oregon, but we saw Mount Shasta and it was like a magnet. It just pulled inside of me and I said to Ann, "Honey, this is it. We're not leaving." The Lord in His infinite wisdom has kept me here through four sawmill closures.

If anyone takes the mountain for granted, I feel sorry for that person. I don't take it for granted. Not a day goes by that I don't look at it and think about it. Being up on the mountain is stress relief for me. I do a lot of praying up there, too.

# Flannery McFadden

"Asking me what I think about Mount Shasta is like asking a fish what it thinks about water," says writer Flannery McFadden. "It's been so much a part of my life that, truthfully, I didn't notice it until I moved away and found that I missed it."

Flannery, 47, was born in Yreka and reared in Hawkinsville, a one-street town on the outskirts of the county seat. After attending Siskiyou County schools, she earned a bachelor's degree in art history from California State University at Sacramento, and a master's degree in psychology from Southern Oregon State College in Ashland.

"When I went away to school, I was never ever going to come back to this 'podunk' place," says Flannery. "I imagined myself in New York City. I came back for one more summer to earn money for a trip to Europe, and I've been here ever since."

Flannery said she went public with her poetry about eight years ago, and is currently working on a book that explores a piece of Siskiyou County history. The following poem is one of many she has written about Mount Shasta.

## I Am A Volcan

*These blue–furred Sierras resent the giant who rides
over my right shoulder. Even Whitney envies the burning
mountains. My volcano guards me from pretensions which
crowd lesser, pushed–up peaks. Pavement and progress
peeve a volcano. She'll end the world, take herself along.
It's said a moon of Mars erupts in fountains, but when earth
convulses, volcan councils send avalanches of fire and rock.*

*I come from the land of one mountain. I don't tell her name,
and she does not tell mine. Here, under her rivals, I sleep,
but my skin does not rest. My mountain mocks these pretty peaks
when I dare dream. She is drowsy and dangerous, an old dowager
apt to say anything to anyone. Ice lays glacial memories
upon her. She poses beautiful and immodest—the lovely are never
modest—beauty was never young, never anything but dangerous.*

*Leaving, I looked back for the last time. Reflected in my
rear view mirror, she stood reversed and strange—how she
sees herself in mountain lakes. Like a bride, shocked at her
wedding portrait, I wondered at my oddly unfamiliar love.*

Shari Nordell

Sunrise          Ned Boss →

# Claudia Mansfield

*Born in the Weed Hospital, Claudia Mansfield spent her early childhood in Tennant on Mount Shasta's north-east side, which is where her mother grew up, and where her father worked as a log truck driver for Long Bell Lumber Company.*

*When the timber operation shut down in Tennant in 1957, the family moved to Mount Shasta where Claudia attended grade school until the family moved again, this time to Napa, when she was 10.*

*Claudia eventually trained in Los Angeles as a hairdresser, and although she was living at the opposite end of the state, she always knew that her heart was still in Mount Shasta.*

*At age 24, when she was working at a salon in Davis, Claudia visited Mount Shasta and became reacquainted with a childhood sweetheart she'd first met at age 12. That first meeting took place at Steel Bridge, a bridge that crossed a portion of the upper Sacramento River which is now underwater at Lake Siskiyou.*

*Claudia moved back to Mount Shasta and married her sweetheart, and worked in a salon for five years before buying the business herself.*

*When she steps out the door of her shop in downtown Mount Shasta, she gets a straight–on view of the mountain.*

As I drive to work in the morning, I always make a point of looking up at the mountain. It just knocks me out every day. Then, during the time I'm working, people will come into the shop and say, "You've got to step outside and look at the mountain!" It will be amazing clouds, or maybe a spectacular sunset that they don't want me to miss. And if I get out to take a lunch break, my eyes always go up to the mountain when I step out the door. It's very much a part of my working day, every day.

I have a wonderful clientele who relate to the mountain in many different ways. They either have an outdoor perspective, or a spiritual focus, or they're artistic. None of them takes the mountain for granted.

Sometimes in the summer, when I leave home for work, I put my mountain bike in the back of my truck. Then, after I'm done working, I start riding up the mountain. Going up, my mind is relaxed and calm, and my body is working hard. Coming down is just the opposite; my body is loose and relaxed and my brain is alert and extremely focused as I look for every little piece of gravel, cracks in the pavement, chipmunks on the side of the road, and cars coming around the corner. No matter how often I take this ride, I acknowledge how blessed I am to have this mountain in my backyard.

One day on my way to work this year, after a whole month of continuous winter storms, I caught a glimpse of the mountain and the treeline looked different. That was the first day we all saw this huge new avalanche which sliced through the forest in finger–like cuts.

Recognizing the change in the treeline made me realize how much attention I pay to that mountain. It's like a familiar face in that I notice when things are different up there. I have a sense of the face of the mountain and am aware of the changes in that face over my lifetime.

Things do change on the mountain, but one thing that never changes is my sense of gratitude for living here and the wonderful sense of community that I have found.

Mount Shasta Boulevard                                          Audra Gibson

Gaillardia, Yarrow and Black-eyed Susans

Jane English

Before the 1995 Avalanche

January 1995 Avalanche Tracks

Everitt Highway and Avalanche Debris - September 1995

It is easy to think of Mount Shasta as solid, massive and unchanging, though we all know it is a volcano, and volcanos are very changable mountains.

One morning in January 1995 after over a week of tremendous rains in the valley and snows on the mountain, I looked out my kitchen window as the clouds finally began to clear. Something seemed odd about the mountain as timberline began to show through the clouds. New markings had appeared. I got an older photograph and compared it with what I saw. The mountain had indeed changed! Over the next days and weeks there were reports of numerous avalanches where there had been none for hundreds of years. Massive old red firs had been tossed around like matchsticks.

So much for our unchanging landmark!

Text and photographs (both pages)    Jane English

## Or Apperson

*When Orbell Apperson was born on the kitchen table in 1923, he was born into a newspaper family.*

*His grandfather, John Apperson, had gone broke with a newspaper in Willows, and heard there was a newspaper called the Sisson Headlight for sale. So he bought it — for $400 in the summer of 1915.*

*Soon Or's dad, also named Orbell, went to work at the Headlight. The elder Apperson died the next winter, leaving his son with the responsibility of a newspaper at the age of 20. Or spent enough of his childhood around the office that he learned to love the smell of ink himself. He left Mount Shasta in 1938 to attend military school, earn a junior college degree, and serve in the Army. In 1946 he enrolled at Stanford University, where he earned a degree in journalism two years later.*

*Or was married in 1949, and in 1950 he and his wife bought the home-town newspaper, now called the Mount Shasta Herald. They bought the Weed Press in 1970, and in 1977 purchased the Dunsmuir News, Weed News, and Siskiyou Advertiser. The papers were sold in 1993 to the American Publishing Company.*

*The Mount Shasta story that Or wants told, "for the record," is the building of the Everitt Memorial Highway, the road that curves its way up the flank of the mountain to the 8,000 foot elevation mark.*

Ski Bowl construction 1958                    Ted Graves

My grandfather wrote an editorial in the Headlight in 1915 that said what Sisson needed most was a wagon road up to Horse Camp, which at that time was the highest place on the mountain to find water for grazing horses. From the time I can first remember, the obsession was to open the mountain to tourists, which we called "visitors" back then. Thus began the Mount Shasta Snowline Highway Project, which was written up in the Sacramento Bee, San Francisco Examiner, and Los Angeles Times.

Skiing brought some people to town, but it was a spectator sport back then. There was a Class A 100–meter jump at Snowman Hill, and people would take the train from Oakland, sleep overnight in the rail cars, and then be taken by the McCloud River Railroad up near Snowman Hill. They'd still have to walk half a mile to watch the ski jumping. The Mount Shasta Chamber of Commerce realized that if a road could be built up the mountain, it would be possible to build a few ski areas along it, as was being done in the Sierra Nevada range.

The highway was begun in 1930 and finished in 1942—but it never went to Horse Camp. The Chamber paid for a survey in 1928, and the road was routed into Sand Flat and back out. That part of the road is still there. The county built the road as far as McBride Springs. The U.S. Forest Service completed the road the rest of the way, taking it on in small segments. The principle dirt moving equipment was a two–horse fresno, which we thought was great, but it's nothing compared to what they have today. They also used a helluva lot of dynamite up there to loosen the dirt because

Everitt Highway in the 1940's                    Ted Graves

a fresno wouldn't work on packed dirt. The whole project took a lot of work. In those days, if you'd have stood up and said you didn't want that highway, you'd have been lynched. It was a religion in this town. It was named after John Everitt, a U.S. Forest Service supervisor who was killed in a fire on the mountain in 1935.

The next project, after World War II, was to get the highway paved. After some heavy politicking by then–Senator Randolph Collier, Forest Highway System funds were earmarked for the paving of the road. In 1956 the first seven miles were built, and the rest was completed the following summer. In the meantime, skiing was really booming. Squaw Valley in the Sierras had a chairlift, and smaller resorts were cropping up all over. A group of 15 local businessmen formed what they called the Chairlift Committee. They surveyed Panther Meadow, and in 1955 formed Mount Shasta Ski Bowl, Inc., which raised $500,000 by selling stock, all locally. They wanted to open the ski area before the 1960 Winter Olympics, which were held at Squaw Valley. The group wanted to attract displaced skiers who would be looking for places to go.

The Mount Shasta Ski Bowl opened for skiing in January of 1958. It didn't even snow until January that first year, and when it did snow, it really dumped a lot. There were 12 feet of snow on the ground at the lodge.

Twenty years later, in January 1978, an avalanche wiped out one of the lifts, and the Ski Bowl never opened again.

Rotary plow on Everitt Highway 1978

Ted Graves

# Elmer Zimmerman

**I**f there's a job connected with the timber industry, Elmer Zimmerman has done it—and always within sight of Mount Shasta.

Elmer was born in 1910 in Iowa City, Iowa and spent his late teen years driving across the country in a Model T Ford, working odd jobs where he found them.

"I stopped in Weed to see my brother, a Cat operator, and he told me that Long Bell Lumber Company was putting on a few men at the time. He convinced me to stay," Elmer said.

In timber harvesting, a tree faller gets the tree to the ground and then its limbs are cut off. Next it is "bucked," or sawn into standard log lengths. A choker–setter runs a cable around the log so it can be dragged to the landing, and in the early days it was a steam loader that hoisted the logs onto a railroad car to be hauled to the mill.

Elmer eventually worked all of these jobs—and more. He was a "Cat doctor," or mechanic at one time, then worked as a foreman running a crew. He worked his way up to camp foreman, and in 1948 became the Long Bell superintendent in Tennant.

Elmer recalls that the rail line dead–ended at Military Pass on Mount Shasta's northerly slopes, so that's the highest Long Bell ever logged on the mountain, to his knowledge. In his first two months of working in the woods, Elmer and other timber workers lived in Tennant and were shuttled by rail to the timber cutting site. But most of the time Elmer worked out of logging camps, which were like mini–cities housing 225 men.

Men in the logging camp would get up at 5 a.m. and eat a meal of hot and cold cereal, bacon and eggs, hot cakes and coffee. "They served good meals all the time, and you could eat all you wanted," said Elmer. The men would then pile into a boxcar that had been modified for transportation with the addition of double walls, seats and windows, and a big wood–burning stove.

A half–hour lunch break was taken during the day, and the hard–working men devoured sack lunches containing three sandwiches, fruit, and pie and cake. They'd work an eight–hour day before returning to camp where they'd eat dinner—two kinds of meat, vegetables, bread, and dessert.

At camp the men stayed in two–person cabins, ate in a mess hall, and showered in a bath house. Elmer remembers that when they came in at the end of the day, there was never quite enough hot water for all of the men to shower immediately.

He tells the story of a "slightly unstable" man we'll call Wild Bob, who was determined to get the first shower every night. Before work, Wild Bob would pack a navy blue duffle bag with his evening clothes and carry it onto the boxcar. When the train pulled into camp at the end of the day, Wild Bob would strip down naked, climb out the window, and hang on the outside of the boxcar until the train was going slow enough for him to jump off and dash to the bath house.

"One night some of the company big wheels and their wives came out, which was unusual because there were hardly ever women in the camp," Elmer said. "They were sitting on the front porch of the commissary when the train came in, and there went Wild Bob streaking naked across the camp. After that we got an order from the company manager Jude White that there would be no more running around naked in camp."

The camps had their wild and woolly sides, to be sure. On payday the prostitutes paid a visit, and every Saturday night the bootleggers arrived with booze to sell. "There was a lot of drinking on Sunday, and some men didn't make it to work on Monday," Elmer said.

Elmer was the marrying type, and he met his future bride during a trip into Tennant. "He came to town, and I saw him, and I thought that was all right," remembers his wife Gladys, who moved to Tennant when she was 10 years old. They were married in 1933 when Elmer was 23 and Gladys was 19.

When Elmer became the superintendent in 1948, he worked out of the Tennant office. He retired in 1972, which is when he and Gladys decided to make their home in Weed. That's where they live today.

Jane English

Elmer maintains a "timber perspective" on the mountain. "I can see Mount Shasta as a continual timber supply if it's handled right," he said. "The timber does grow slowly up there, and although it's an awfully hard thing for anybody to have a hard and fast rule on the type of cutting they should do up there, I'm not in favor of clear–cutting on the mountain at all. You need seed trees, and shade for trees that are coming along."

Gladys has her own way of looking at Mount Shasta: "We used to travel a lot, and when we'd be gone two or three months I'd start thinking about the mountain. I just couldn't wait to see it again."

Anthony Colburn

# Orvis Agee

"Not bad for a guy who's just a bunch of bones held together with rubber bands."

That's how Orvis Freeland Agee describes himself.

Orvis, a resident of Woodland, California may be the oldest man to have climbed Mount Shasta. He was 85 (and a half) years old on his last ascent of the mountain which took place on July 10, 1988. Even more impressive is the fact that exactly a week earlier he had climbed Mount Lassen in one day, and ten days after the Shasta climb he scaled California's highest peak—Mount Whitney.

"You do things an older man doesn't usually do and you get a lot of attention," he said with a wink during a 1994 interview in his home. "I guess I used to float up mountains on that kind of praise."

Shasta isn't the only mountain that called Orvis' name. He was recently honored by the American Lung Association for raising $120,000 over 18 years by joining annual 100–mile fundraising hikes through the Sierra Nevada range.

"The first year I did the 100–mile lung association trip was in 1974, and they were reluctant to let me join the group because I was 71 years old,"

Orvis said. "I was finally allowed to go when I explained that I had climbed Mount Shasta three times the previous year. Still, they assigned a big burley guy to follow me, and he complained because he couldn't keep me in sight."

Born on January 11, 1903, Orvis caught his first sight of Mount Shasta at age 11 when his family moved to the Fall River Valley about an hour's drive east of the mountain.

He remembers watching the 1915 eruption of Mount Lassen while he and his sister Irene were cultivating an orchard.

"We saw the explosion shooting in the air, and the next day it smelled like sulfur and a light ash fell around us," he said.

But it was Mount Shasta that struck his fancy.

"One winter afternoon in 1916 when I was 13 years old, my sister and younger brother and I rode our horses to the foot of Soldier Mountain, which rises 1,100 feet above the valley floor. We tied the horses to trees and tried climbing the steep mountain side. I walked ahead, breaking trail. Two and half hours later we reached the summit. We could see the full height of Mount Shasta. We came down in 20 minutes, making long leaps in the soft, steep snow.

"I loved Mount Shasta so much," Orvis said. "It was such a pretty thing way out there beyond the next mountain range. But the idea of climbing Mount Shasta never occurred to me. It seemed like some sacred thing that one worshiped from afar."

It was his son Philip who, at age nine, suggested the climb. In 1962, after three tries, Orvis Agee stood triumphant on the summit of Mount Shasta. Orvis was four months shy of age 60 on that climb.

Over the years he made 39 attempts at Shasta's summit, 30 of which were successful.

"Every time I had different people with me," he said. "One time I had 24 Sierra Club members from Davis with me, and 21 more from Reno. That was a lot of people to look after. I don't know why, but other people always wanted to climb with me."

Working as a house builder and woodworker in a relatively flat, rural area, Orvis trained for his climbs by hoofing it up and down the stairs at the seven–story Woodland Memorial Hospital.

What inspired him? What moved him up the steep and sometimes perilous trail? What kept him ever seeking that craggy Shasta summit?

Orvis answers: "It's just so darned much fun."

Jeffrey Rich

Shasta's Shadow at Sunrise

Michael Zanger

# Rowena Pattee Kryder

*Brochures that promote books and workshops by Rowena Pattee Kryder, M.F.A., Ph.D. describe her as a mother, visionary artist, mythologist, Zen student, spiritual teacher, scholar, author, cinematographer, former faculty member at the California Institute of Integral Studies in San Francisco, and founder of the Creative Harmonics Institute near Weed.*

*But the titles alone do not explain the kind of life led by this 60-year-old woman who has built two non-sectarian temples, started her own publishing company, and produced five animated "cosmic" films. Drawing from visions, studies of mythology and archetypes, and experience, she has, in addition to her books, created two sets of oracle cards, most recently the* Gaia Matrix Oracle. *Publishers Weekly said that her latest book,* Emerald River of Compassion, *"may be* The Celestine Prophesy's New Age match."*

*In 1987, Rowena bought 41 acres of land within view of Mount Shasta. There she designed and built a 12-sided house based on the zodiac. The center of the house is a raised stage used for meditation, teaching, music, and sacred theater. It is here that Rowena continues to study and create.*

*The following are some thoughts offered by Rowena during an interview.*

My main thing is creativity. It doesn't matter the medium. I ask fundamental questions, and I want to know the answers. I'm a highly motivated person, mainly because I feel I have lifetimes of commitment to humanity's future. I'm really interested in where we're going, and in providing some kind of basic foundation where future generations don't have to suffer the way past generations have. It is unnecessary, totally unnecessary, to have so much confusion.

One of my interests in life is giving people the tools and abilities and confidence to be who they are—not who they think they are, but to be completely open to the creative, open to the unknown. You never know what's going to emerge, and that's the joy of it. It's not a question of learning something; it's a question of participating in the mysteries of the universe.

Mount Shasta offers a good place for that investigation because it is such a highly charged place, and a high vibration place. By that I mean that it's a relatively clear place for contemplating, reassessing, and receiving inspiration. I just feel good here. I don't know whether that's due to the mountain, the lack of pollution, or this particular piece of land, which is just full of what the Chinese call "chi," or subtle energy. I find that energy very conducive to health, and health is conducive to raised consciousness, and raised consciousness is conducive to solving problems. So I find it a very nurturing place to receive inspiration. And then I go out in the world from here.

In cities it's harder to be receptive of the inspiration that's going on all the time, everywhere, because of the interference of thought forms, pollution, all kinds of things. The inspiration is always there, even in the city. It's just harder to get through.

Before I moved to this area I had visited friends here repeatedly and had known Mount Shasta for years and years. When I was shown this land, this 40 acres, it was actually the land that spoke to me, the devas of the trees and meadows. It was really like a calling in the sense of being a steward in this particular area. This area, I feel, is a very pristine area and has great potential for what I call a New Earth community. When I'm guided to something, it just works out, so I just go for it. You have to totally enjoy nature and be resourceful and somewhat rugged to live here. It's not an easy process. Everything is harder here, but there's also more joy, more ecstacy.

As for the mountain itself, it is just there, and I'm sitting out to the west of it enjoying it. I haven't climbed it; I'm not very ambitions that way. I'm happy to just be here and let it vibrate and be what it is. The mountain is a central focal point for all of us; we have that in common. We enjoy it in various ways. For me it's a view, it's an inspiration.

Rowena Pattee Kryder

March Storm

Rowena Pattee Kryder

47

*I live in the cradle between the rising raw rocks of Mount Shasta and the forest covered Eddy Mountains, where water bubbles up from the ground. My soul bursts in beauty here, at dawn, noon, evening and by moonlight. I am a creature of history, yet the mountains speak in an older tongue.*

᪥ ᪥ ᪥ ᪥ ᪥

*Shastina is a heart, the open female, nestled in the higher peak of Mount Shasta. Gods and goddesses live in their crevices and crags, seeking to perfect their relationships. Sometimes they get intoxicated on the spirits of snowflakes that flutter down at night as they make love.*

᪥ ᪥ ᪥ ᪥ ᪥

*White purity, dark penetration -*
*The shining jewel of Mount Shasta is home, wherever I am.*

᪥ ᪥ ᪥ ᪥ ᪥

*Announced by the violet darkness glowing in the east, the sun rises. The dawn shimmers across a veil that enlivens the river of the sky over the profile of the mountain. Mount Shasta is unperturbed, silent, fixed like a stubborn donkey.*

᪥ ᪥ ᪥ ᪥ ᪥

*Winds of the south, blown through the nostrils of hoary old spirits, enliven my fragile time in the mountains. Volcanic fire snakes underground as my small feet tread lightly on the trail to Squaw Valley. My blood feels the lava. My breath knows the storm. When I grow weary I crawl up in the uterus of the earth and rest inside Mount Shasta.*

# Elden Hoy

Elden Hoy enjoys a spectacular view of Mount Shasta from his 950–acre cattle ranch just outside of Weed. But that's about the extent of Elden's interest in his volcanic neighbor on the horizon.

Dressed in jeans, cowboy boots, a button down shirt and suspenders, he takes a pull on a cigarette and says, "I grew up and it was just there, just part of the country. Now I look up there to see what the weather is doing. If there's snow blowing from north to south, then I know the wind is blowing from the city of Mount Shasta down to Sacramento."

Those sentiments don't reflect the rich ranching life led at the foot of the mountain by 75–year–old Elden, his son Bill, and Elden's father, the late Albertis "Bert" Hoy. It was Bert who bought what is now the Hoy Hereford Ranch in 1916.

Bert was six weeks old when his family moved from Kansas to Red Bluff in 1877. Thirty–two years later, in 1909, he and his brother Mart moved to Siskiyou County. Bert married Nora Rucker in 1915, and the couple lived in Edgewood for a year before buying what is now the Hoy ranch in 1916. In 1921 Bert recognized the future of top Hereford cattle and purchased his first registered stock. To this day it's the oldest registered herd in Siskiyou County, and the second oldest in the state.

In 1920 Bert and Nora had a son, Elden, born in Nora's mother's home, which was the Arbaugh Ranch at that time.

Elden's son Bill Hoy has been dubbed "the family historian" because he has a neatly–kept photo album full of marriage licenses, letters from the 1800s, birth certificates, and photographs of the rugged men and women in the family's past. But it is Elden who tells the tales, and who remembers the details of early ranching life at the foot of the mountain.

The family has a splendid picture of Bert Hoy perched on the summit of Mount Shasta, taken sometime between 1910 and 1915. He is wearing long pants, a long–sleeved shirt, suspenders and a hat, and is holding a long walking stick. His cow dog is perched at his feet.

"They left Weed on horseback and rode as high as they could," said Elden, using words to color in the black and white photo. "It was my dad, his sister, her husband, and an uncle who went on the climb. On the way up there they shot a couple of bucks, hung them up, and picked them up on the way back."

In those days, Bert Hoy let his cattle spend the summer on free pasture land near McCloud. They'd grow hay at the ranch while the cattle were away, and then herd them back for the winter. One July, while the herd was near McCloud, it snowed so much that the cattle, thinking it was winter, returned on their own to the Hoy Ranch.

"They had to herd them all the way back to McCloud," Elden chuckled.

Some of his earliest memories are of the colorful characters that his parents would hire to help out during haying season. Most of the time they were Irish migrant workers who were hard–working and hard–drinking. They'd arrive on a freight train and stay in bunkhouses provided by the ranchers.

"My first job was plucking chickens to feed everybody," Elden said. "I can smell chicken soup today, and all I smell is wet feathers. If you try it for awhile, you will, too."

He also remembers the time a crew of rowdy workers convinced his mother to let them take 12–year–old Elden to town with them to see a movie. They introduced him to the local "cat house" instead.

Elden's social life in his later teen years consisted mainly of attending dances at the Hippodrome in Weed, Joyland in Dunsmuir, and Branstetter Hall in McCloud.

"I can remember during haying season going to dances that lasted until three in the morning," he said. "I'd get home just in time to change my clothes, eat my breakfast, and go to work. Dad never cared how long I stayed

out as long as I got the work done. Sometimes the day got a little long before it was over, but I survived."

Elden married Betty Lester in 1942, and in 1944 their son Bill was born in the Weed Hospital. Bill also attended Weed schools and earned an associate arts degree at College of the Siskiyous before going on to study entomology at the University of California at Davis. He was 10 units shy of a degree when his dad's main ranch hand became ill, and Bill returned home to help his father.

"I've been here ever since," he said.

Bill says that thick brush prevents cattle from grazing much on Mount Shasta; the Hoys keep their herd on the ranch year–round now.

"My grandfather climbed Mount Shasta, my dad climbed Black Butte, and I've climbed the hill behind the house here," Bill said. "I enjoy looking at Mount Shasta. I'm always glad to get home to it. It's like an old friend: you can always count on it."

Anthony Colburn

51

## Jim Nile

Come take a walk around Mount Shasta with Jim Nile, a retired forester who formerly managed timber stands for a company that was the largest private landowner in California.

Jim grew up in Nevada County and later attended the University of California at Berkeley where he earned a degree in forestry in 1952. His first job was in Siskiyou and Shasta counties, cruising timber on the Hearst Estate at Wyntoon.

Later that year, Southern Pacific Land Company started a forest management program and wanted to hire someone with timber cruising experience. Jim was brought on board as assistant district forester, and helped to manage 200,000 acres in Siskiyou, north Shasta, and northeast Trinity counties. A fair number of those acres were on the slopes of Mount Shasta, Jim said.

In 1983 there was a merger of Santa Fe and Southern Pacific corporations, and the land holdings were combined to create Santa Fe Pacific Timber Company, with headquarters in Redding. Jim worked there for nine years before retiring in January of 1988. At about the time he retired, the company's landholdings were sold to Sierra Pacific Industries, making SPI the largest private landowner in the state.

Back in 1952, when Jim took the job, the first order of business was to take inventory of the timber on company lands. The company began its management program by logging in the McCloud Flats area—prime terrain where trees grow well.

"The McCloud side of the mountain has the best timber—in the upper Squaw Valley Creek drainage, Mud Creek drainage, Pilgrim Creek, and Cold Creek," Jim said.

"Our entry into a forest was always to solve mortality problems —spike-top trees, fire scars at the butt, biological problems, or insect infestation," he said. "Our first effort was to reduce mortality and get a road system established. We marked all the trees to be logged, then we let a timber sale contract to a sawmill. They in turn usually hired a logging and road construction company. SP supervised as landowner."

In 1954 the company logged Red Fir in the Squaw Valley Creek area, and the south side of Red Butte, doing what Jim called "a very sensitive job of cutting."

"The south side has wonderful stands of Shasta Red Fir that are high in quality and readily logged, and reproduce nicely," he said. "There were very few management problems there. Those areas require light logging because if you open up the forest too much, the trees that are left can blow down easily because of the light volcanic soil and rotting characteristics of that tree species. Since most of the precipitation that falls on the mountain is in the form of snow, you get few erosion problems; as always a diligent job of erosion prevention is essential."

Jim & Velma—the day he proposed!
photo by Gino Trevisan

The company then continued logging around to the east and north sides of the mountain

"The quality of timber is lower on those sides because of lower precipitation," Jim explained. "The productivity of the land is lower, the trees aren't as tall, and they have lots of limbs. We were cutting trees that were 500 years old because in some areas it takes 40 years to put an inch on the circumference of a tree. We logged up to 7,000 feet on the north side, but it's just not ideally suited to long–term management. It has a short growing season."

Jim says he enjoyed working for the company that hired him, and that he especially relished working on Mount Shasta.

"I liked being up there," he said. "You have these open forest stands without a lot of brush underneath. In the summertime when it was hot everywhere else, it was pleasant up there.

"I believe that overall our company did a careful, sensitive job of cutting trees. In the 1980s, the forward–looking land exchange program resulted in the exchange of many of the company's high elevation lands for forest management lands elsewhere," Jim said. "I have always been what might be called 'productivity oriented.' I believe in growing things, good stewardship, and in multiple use. Our forests should be managed for uses. The current trend is to stress other values. But there's enough opportunity with good stewardship to accommodate all uses. I truly believe that."

In Jim's case, 'multiple use' applies to marriage proposals. It was on the summit of Mount Shasta in 1955 that he asked Velma Little to be his wife. It was Velma's first time to climb the mountain.

"We had been on the summit for awhile, and then I popped the question," he said. He received an affirmative answer, even though he says he wasn't confident enough to carry an engagement ring to the top.

"It just seemed like a good place to propose," Jim said. "You don't want to propose marriage when you're going out to the dump or some other mundane thing. You want a special occasion, and standing on the summit of Mount Shasta was a special occasion."

Michael Zanger

# *Velma Nile*

Hundreds and hundreds of people have fond memories of learning to ski on Mount Shasta — thanks to an army of volunteers and a program that offered low–cost lessons from 1953 to 1970.

For most of the program's 17–year life, Velma Nile was the director under the auspices of the Mount Shasta Recreation District. Because of sponsorship help from the local newspaper in the second year, it was called the Mount Shasta Herald Ski School.

For the first four years the school was held using the surface lift at Snowman Hill on the summit of Highway 89 between the towns of Mount Shasta and McCloud. One dollar bought six Saturday lessons, and children came from all over the south county to learn.

"It seems everyone in town got involved in the program," said Velma, who was the overseer of as many as 80 volunteer instructors and aides. "They searched their barns and attics for any ski equipment they had. Kids came onto the hill wearing an amazing assortment of gear. Some had long, home–made skis and others had new ones from Montgomery Wards with leather straps."

Groups of 8 to 10 students were organized each Saturday using big signs and a battery–operated public address system, Velma said. The classes were open to students in fourth grade through high school, unless their parents were instructors, in which case younger children were accepted.

In the winter of 1957–58 the ski school program moved up to the new Mt. Shasta Ski Bowl, which brought some changes to the operation. The student population increased, with youths being bussed in from Yreka, Tulelake, and Burney. Velma remembers the parking lot being full of buses. In the peak years, she said, there were as many as 600 children enrolled.

The move to the Ski Bowl brought other changes as well—mainly with weather conditions.

"We found there were some Saturdays that you just couldn't put kids on the mountain," said Velma. "We'd try to decide by 6 a.m., and then call the local radio station to get out the word about whether lessons would be held or canceled. Sometimes we'd sit in the lodge and watch the wind gauge hit 100 miles per hour."

She remembers, too, playing music on the PA system at the bottom of the hill so that on foggy days the young skiers would know which way was down.

Velma said she has nothing but good memories of the ski school, the officials and business people with whom she worked, the volunteers, and the children who learned to ski there.

"Everyone worked really hard because we all loved to ski," she said. "They were all anxious to share what they knew about skiing. As soon as some of the kids reached the top level, then they became instructors, so we produced our own teachers in a cycle. I so appreciated the cooperation among the volunteers and their willingness to put in long hours."

The Mount Shasta Herald Ski School came to an end in 1970 by mutual agreement of those involved.

"I never really stopped to think about why I did it," said Velma. "I guess it was just fun, and it's all right to do fun things. Also, I have always worked with children, whether it's teaching swimming or taking them backpacking. I just got my first fishing license so I could take my grandson fishing."

She still likes to ski, too, and as a one–time biology instructor enjoys getting on Mount Shasta to observe the plant life there.

Velma also savors the mountain from afar.

"I like the changes in light on the mountain," she said. "It's best in the early morning or late afternoon. I never get up and look out the window without feeling glad that I live here. It's home."

Ski School at the Snow Bowl - 1959    Ted Graves                    Lake Siskiyou    Jane English →

# Robert Webb

*The man who holds the record for the fastest ascent of Mount Shasta got his first taste of climbing in the eastern states. Robert Webb was born in Vermont, and by the time he was 14 he had climbed 46 peaks over 4,000 feet in the Adirondacks. He made his first winter ascent of a mountain at age 6. He climbed later in South America, Nepal, and Alaska.*

*As of 1995 Robert has been the caretaker at the Sierra Club cabin at Horse Camp for 13 years. He also guides treks and climbs in California, and in other mountainous regions in the world.*

*Here is the story of his love for the mountain, and his record–breaking climb.*

Mount Shasta has always fascinated me, even when I first sensed her magnitude when I saw her in an atlas. I was 20 then and first climbed to her summit in 1978. I will never forget that first climb, surging up through the Red Banks at 13,000 feet, my heart like thunder in my chest, my thighs burning and my breath raging like wild fire. To feel so high above the world, to see the myriad of blues and greens in the valley below blending into the fall horizon, and to have every fiber in my body screaming with the exertion and pure air, put me into another dimension I will never forget.

I returned to Mount Shasta four years later, in 1982, to climb the mountain again. I never left Shasta after that second trip; I ended up as caretaker at Horse Camp.

I had never before lived in a place where I felt so alive and energized. While many quicken in the womb, I quickened inside Shasta. In the way a mountain chickadee song pierces the stillness, the mountain changed my life forever.

When I think back to the time period leading up to doing the fast climbs, culminating in my 99–minute run to the top, it may sound strange but it all seemed to happen easily. Not that there wasn't any effort or sweat involved. It was just that my body seemed to want the stress and exertion to push myself to the limits. The training involved running up the nearby arm of Casaval Ridge, or going up to Helen Lake at 10,400 feet, or doing some trail running. I would push myself, but it didn't seem like work; I would go just as far as my body would let me. It was as if I could relax knowing that I was going to use every ounce of energy I had to propel me up the slope, and with this knowledge I would surrender my body to my will to drive me upwards as fast as the machine of my body would allow.

To me, running up the mountain was an expression of my sheer appreciation of all the magic and energy which seemed to surround Mount Shasta.

The first climb I did in under two hours was in 1 hour and 58 minutes. I remember breaking out onto the summit plateau knowing that I had already broken the old record easily. The sight of the summit was beautiful and even in my full–on dash across the snow, with my breaths coming fast and furious in my head, I could feel the deep serenity and peace of the mountain pervade me. The second speed climb was accomplished in 1 hour and 47 minutes.

I climbed the mountain in a record 1 hour and 39 minutes on July 5, 1985—60 years to the day after David Lawyer set the previous record of 2 hours and 24 minutes in 1925.

Two days previous to the climb I went to the summit to stash a packload of water, food, warm clothing, and heavier boots for the descent. On the morning of the climb I got up and drank a lot of peppermint tea with maple syrup and did 45–minutes of yoga stretching and deep breathing. This got my body relaxed and the energy flowing. I made up a big batch of whole–grain pancakes and ate a stack with maple syrup to get well carbed–up.

For the climb I wore polypropylene long johns, a t–shirt, lightweight hiking boots, and a waist pack containing light clothing, water, and a little food. I carried ski poles for extra traction on the steep sections.

The starting time was set at 9:30 a.m. and there were three synchronized watches: two held by the timers at the base and summit, and I wore the third. The starting line was strung from the corner of the cabin to the spring. I approached the starting line at a full run so that when the line dropped I was already up to speed.

I was able to run as far as Spring Hill, then I went into my scrambling–walk mode that I used on most of the climb, where I would find footholds and move from one to the next in a fluid motion, using the ski poles for extra thrust and balance. I became so absorbed in my own breathing, working on how to get the most out of each breath and how to draw the most out of every footfall and the frame of my body, that each step became an experience in itself. People that I passed along the way said I gave them the sensation of moving backwards.

Most of the route was covered with firm snow with plenty of divots (sun cups) for footholds. The chutes through Red Banks were icy but I used the edge of the rock for traction and a couple of footholds chopped in the ice by the timer who had gone up ahead of me. Around Red Banks it got cold and windy so I put on a hat and windbreaker I had in my pack while I kept moving. I dumped out my remaining quart of water to get rid of extra weight.

Cresting out over Misery Hill was an elating experience. I felt a surge of happiness to see the summit goal so near. I saw the beauty in all the jumbled rocks and sculpted snow and felt so high, as if I could reach up to the heavens, one tiny speck interacting with infinity. I ran across the summit plateau as fast as I could. I remember climbing the pinnacle thinking to myself, "I can't believe I am pushing myself this hard." At one point I faltered, almost to a stop; I wanted so much to catch my breath.

After I reached the summit I coughed violently for a couple of minutes, then felt fine. I put on all the clothes I had because it was cold and windy.

I had no idea what kind of time I could make within what was such a profound experience. I guess it was all part of the wonder and feeling of amazement to be able to live on a mountain as holy and giving as Shasta.

Coming down I took my time, and it took over two hours—longer than the 99–minute climb up.

The fire I feel inside for this mountain will always burn, flicker, and glow. It's as if my system is permanently infused with the presence of the mountain which flows in my blood. Once I had drunk of her cup I was bewitched for life. I will be carried on her song, and my heart is eternally uplifted. Every morning I go to the spring and douse my face in the ice cold waters, close my eyes, feel the sting and power in the water as it washes away the last shreds of sleep, and give thanks for this purity of life.

Gerhard Bock

Ascent                    Michael Zanger

How many times I climbed Mount Shasta with my eyes and in my heart before I made that first ascent!
—*Marie Mitchell*

The summit is reached one breath-filled step at a time.  Going higher and higher means reaching deeper and deeper into inner reserves of faith, energy, essence. It is a purification by the fire of one's own Being.
A Sacred Journey... A transformative adventure.
— *Marie Mitchell*

Now at last I see
The peak is meant for God,
The climb for me
— *Anonymous*
(seen painted on a boulder during a 1954 climb)

Descent                    Anthony Colburn

When I am here on this mountain, I am reminded that there is greater significance to this physical existence than what meets the eye, and I am turned in to my own revelation of Godliness.
— *Anonymous climber*
(Mount Shasta summit register 1971)

Climbers Camp — Lake Helen                    George Stroud

58

John Jackson

# Tom Pinkson

*Tom Pinkson was born in the heart of New York City in 1945. The death of his father when Tom was four years old set him on a path of exploration that began with psychosomatic illness and juvenile delinquency, but eventually took him to numerous shamanic Medicine Teachers and an eleven year apprenticeship with a group of Huichol Indian shamans of north-central Mexico.*

*During this time, Tom earned three college degrees, including a Ph.D. in psychology. His doctoral dissertation, "A Quest for Vision," described his successful work with heroin addicts in the early 1970's using a wilderness treatment program in the Sierras. He went on to help start one of the first hospice programs in the United States.*

*Walking in two worlds, the shamanic world of indigenous spirituality and the Western world of a practicing psychologist, public-speaker and high-performance coach to business executives and health professionals, Tom serves as a bridge builder, bringing what he calls The Teachings of the Elders into practical applications within modern business settings.*

*Tom, whose recent book is* Flowers of Wiricuta: A Gringo's Journey to Shamanic Power, *has two grown children and lives with his wife, Andrea, a pediatric nurse, in San Rafael, California.*

*The following is an excerpt from the book.*

I first came to Mount Shasta on a car camping trip with my family. In the dark at one in the morning, we parked our VW bus at the end of the road and tried to fall asleep on its floor. But I could not. I felt a huge presence looming behind me, an energy field that would not let me do anything except know its power. Finally, I dozed off, only to be awakened at first light by the sound of clanking metal. Peering out the window into the rising mist, I saw two figures walking past with ice axes and crampons swinging from their shoulders. *Ah, they're climbers,* I thought. A surge of excitement shot through me. *I've got to come back someday and climb here, too. I've got to go to the source of power.* I crawled out of my sleeping bag, opened the door of the bus and stepped out into the frigid air. I looked directly ahead and there it was; looming higher and higher into the sky, it looked endless. As the first rays of light illuminated its snow-covered shimmering white beauty, I fell in love.

Since that time, I have returned to this magnificent holy place on a regular basis. It has become a yearly pilgrimage that I make with a group of twelve people who have been working with me for a year in a shamanic healing and empowerment group. We go to the mountain with the goal of climbing as high as we can as a team. But high is measured not just in physical terms; it is also measured in terms of how we stay in touch with each other—with hearts and spirits opened and united.

A Mount Shasta pilgrimage in 1993 with members of the year-long healing group brought teachings that had been sneaking up on me for quite a while. They had to do with my new understanding of power. Early conditioning as a male in this culture is always about pushing harder to get what you want. So I did just that with weight training, running marathons and mountain climbing. But even though I trained hard to be in good cardiovascular condition with plenty of physical strength as well, I'd still get tired every time I went mountain climbing, tired enough to be unable to fully enjoy being there. This climb changed my whole drive-push pattern. Now I know I can still push when I need to, and sometimes that is precisely what is needed in a given situation, but I have found a much better way to accomplish my goals, both in the mountains as well as back here in the lowlands.

The night before the climb, the group gathered around the fire. We were in our base camp at 9,600 feet. The stars were sparkling like diamonds in the rarefied high-mountain air. The temperature was below freezing and dropping fast. We huddled inside our parkas, leaning against each other for added warmth. I took out my drum and warmed it near the flames.

I prayed aloud, then listened to the prayers of the eleven other members of our pilgrimage. When each person had spoken, I picked up my now warmed drum and said, "Now is the time for us to call in our power animals." The beat of the drum began slowly. After a while, I felt an energy pouring into me. It was playing the drum by itself, as though I were the one being drummed. I closed my eyes and called in Kauyumari, the Deer Spirit. *Thank you, Kauyumari, for all you do for me helping me on my path. I appreciate you and I love you. I want you to go up on the mountain and ask what is most important for me to be aware of tomorrow. Ask for wisdom guidance. Ho, thank you, Kauyumari.*

I felt Kauyumari enter my body and whisk my spirit up to the heights. I expected to go to the summit. To my surprise, Kauyumari took me right into the center of the mountain. There I saw the heart of the little spirit the Creator placed within Mount Shasta. My awareness went straight into her, blending and joining until there was no sense of "me." Then I heard her speak: *Listen to my heartbeat, grandson. When you climb tomorrow, go slow enough so that you can stay in touch with my beating heart with each step. Don't get ahead of me. I will give you heart. You do not have to climb the mountain by yourself. To try to do so will be a mistake. You are never alone. Your strength is puny compared to the strength of the forces that created me. Keep your heart open and connected to mine. Sing your Deer Song. Kauyumari will carry you up the mountain on its back. But only if you stay with my heartbeat.*

Three o'clock in the morning came very quickly. I woke the others, had a quick hot breakfast, and by four o'clock we were on our way with flashlights and moonlight to guide our steps. I tried my best to follow the instructions I had been given the previous evening. I used the pounding of my heart to remind me to stay open to the heartbeat of the little mountain spirit. I sang the Huichol Deer Song silently as we snaked our way up the mountain.

Eight hours later, I stood atop the summit with five others. Tears flowing, wind blasting, we hugged each other and offered our prayers up to the Great Spirit and the powers of creation. There was nothing above us but the free space of the heavens. The landscape spread out below us for hundreds of miles.

I took stock of my feelings: elation, exhilaration, and gratitude to all the members of our group and to all those who had come before. In the midst of all this jubilation, I was delighted to notice that I felt no fatigue whatsoever. On other climbs, I'd been elated to reach the summit but was exhausted as well. This time, there was no fatigue, no aching muscles.

*I've got to remember this, I thought. I need to bring Kauyumari into all the mountains of my life. No more climbing alone. This is the way to do it— with spirit leading the way and me following. Spirit's got infinite juice; mine is drastically limited.*

Jane English

61

## Felice Steele

Felice Steele is giving serious consideration to her feelings about life at the foot of Mount Shasta while she pets the family cat curled up in her lap. The cat does not distract her in the least; Felice is a 13–year–old who can focus.

Born in Mount Shasta in 1982, she has been home–schooled all of her life. At age 9 she took classes in Voice and Fundamentals of Music at College of the Siskiyous, and she continues to augment her education with other COS classes.

As part of a study unit assigned by her mother, Felice researched everything she could find about volcanos, and the family even paid a visit to Mount St. Helens, which had just recently erupted.

"It freaked me out for a year," said Felice who was five at the time. "Every time after that when there was an earthquake, I'd flip out that we were feeling warning shakes before the mountain erupted. I'd start to pace and turn on the news. Mom assigned me to put together an emergency kit so we'll be prepared for an eruption or some other catastrophe. There are two bins in it — one for our family and one for our animals. The one for the family has a lot of food in it, and a first aid kit. The other one has food, kitty litter, leashes.

"The idea of an eruption doesn't freak me out so much now," Felice said. "Now I realize that I'm a lot happier living with a volcano than I would be with a flood plain or something."

Jane English

Aside from the threat posed by the volcanic nature of Mount Shasta, Felice is undecided about the mountain's role in her life.

"Mount Shasta has been there my whole life, so I don't pay much attention to it," she said. "Every so often in the winter I ski on it. I like Mount Shasta best in the winter when it's really snowy. And when the mountain is especially pretty I'll look at it and think about how lucky I am to live next to something like that.

"It's weird, but, when I go to flat places like Indiana, where my dad grew up, it feels really strange not to have the mountain there," Felice said. "I could probably go for days without looking at it and it would be no big deal. But after a while, I know I would miss it. That's the weird thing: I've thought and thought about why that is, but I can't figure it out.

"I'm sure it does affect my life, but I couldn't point out how, or why. Maybe it's just because it's been there my entire life. There's no way something that big could not affect your life, you know?"

Vada Gipson

Jane English

# Marge Apperson

*For the past 45 years, Marge Apperson has maintained a perspective unlike any other on the mountain and its namesake community. After graduating from Stanford University, she moved to Mount Shasta City and served over the years as co–owner, publisher, and editor of the Mount Shasta Herald and other area newspapers until her retirement in 1994.*

*Her reporting ran the gamut of city council meetings, mountain rescues, environmental issues, law enforcement and education matters, and just about anything else that happened in town or on Mount Shasta.*

*Because of her many years in the town and her knowledge of its history, politics, and social structure, Marge was asked to write specifically about the way in which the mountain itself has influenced the community of Mount Shasta.*

Mount Shasta, while drawing admiration and worship for its majestic presence and awesome beauty, in turn has cast its shadow on the town of Mount Shasta in the form of divisiveness since the 1960's.

The very magnetism of spiritual and aesthetic splendor that started the migration to the mountain in the 1960's, primarily to the town at its base, also sparked a conflict that has been ongoing since that day.

The notions, the actions, the political and social views of hippies, environmentalists, New Agers, and a younger, mobile generation automatically came in conflict with the conservative population of Mount Shasta, creating a split that has never healed.

Inject new ideas, ideals and lifestyles into an unsophisticated, stable population based on a timber and lumber mill economy—with many second and third generation families often inter–related—and you have fear and resentment of the new values that come with them.

The arrival of the original hippies in the 1960's—reminiscent of the influx of "Rainbow Family" members in recent years—triggered the conflict that has continued in one way or another to this day. The middle class town, with strong ties to church and family, reacted sharply to the outside influences. Even the mayor carried a sidearm on his hip and had a "no hippies served" sign in his business. The townspeople, sensitized to this unwelcome group, carried over their resentment to the subsequent waves of new populations.

A movement of educated, more sophisticated young people, used to the post–war freedom and mobility, were drawn to Mount Shasta by the mountain and the beauty of the area, arriving with their new ideas. The sexual freedom, different lifestyles, and less emphasis on family values, community service, and church, kept this group within itself, apart from the core population of the town, and thus the schism between the townsfolk and the newcomers became broader and deeper.

Neither side understood, or wanted to understand, the other, and this has maintained the unfriendly relationship between "old Mount Shasta" and the newcomers—the new arrivals—to this day.

The newcomers—environmentalists, members of the younger generation hungering to get away from city life, and those drawn by the spiritual nature of Mount Shasta—had their own agendas that did not include the established way of life in Mount Shasta.

They wanted to change the way things were being done: to save the forests, the wilderness, from the loggers; to establish new ideas, new concepts for how the town itself would develop and look; to have a voice in the politics of the town.

The original population resented the newcomers who were drawn to the beautiful area and the town whose inhabitants were comfortable with things the way they were.

At every step, the old timers rebelled. Factions formed that are active to this day, with one polarized group of old–timers trying to block every new move and a matching group of newcomers taking an intractable course in gaining their objective. At the middle of these extremes are the varying shades of gray—with only a small group truly understanding both views.

Both sides love the beauty of the area, sitting under the majesty of Mount Shasta. And just what gives both sides joy leads to a divided town. Whether the few in the centrist group that understand the views of both sides will succeed in healing the rift has yet to be determined.

Gerhard Bock

California Poppies

# Carl Martin

When the U.S. Forest Service asked for bids to build a ski area on Mount Shasta in 1984, Carl Martin was ecstatic: he saw the project as his ticket home.

The son of a logger and homemaker, Carl was born in Mount Shasta in 1941 and spent most of his growing up years near the Scott Valley town of Callahan. The family frequently visited Mount Shasta.

"Every time my dad had five minutes off, we went to the mountain," said Carl. They spent a lot of time in Panther Meadow and ski bowl areas, he said.

In his teen years, Carl and some friends built a little rope tow ski operation on Salmon Mountain. Anyone who brought a gallon of gas to run the tow was welcome to ski for a week.

By then, a love of skiing ran thick in Carl's blood. When he attended Sierra College in Auburn, he was captain of the ski team, which won the Far West Collegiate Ski Title. He was also president of the school's ski club.

After suffering a foot injury, Carl moved to Mount Shasta in 1961 and finished his associate arts degree at College of the Siskiyous in Weed while coaching the Mount Shasta Ski Bowl Race Team—the Panthers.

He served in the U.S. Army for two years and came home once again, this time to work for the U.S. Forest Service in Callahan doing snow surveys and firefighting. For two years he managed helicopter operations for fires and rescue work in the area.

Then he headed in a different direction.

"When I was a young kid I saw a television commercial where Monte Atwater (a famous skier) kicked an avalanche down a mountain and skied down after it for Miller Time," Carl said. "I was very much impressed by that, so I was very happy to learn that the Forest Service had snow ranger positions."

For the next nine years Carl's snow ranger and resource officer duties took him to Mt. Baldi in Southern California, Willamette Pass in Oregon, and China Peak in the Sierra Nevada range. In 1978 he was assigned to Mammoth Mountain where he worked as director of the Forest Service Avalanche Forecast Center for the southern Sierra range, and was in charge of winter sports operations for June Mountain and Mammoth Mountain .

"By then I had kicked many avalanches down the mountain," Carl laughed.

After 20 years and two days of working for the Forest Service, Carl was hired by Mammoth Mountain resort as a ski area designer, and drew up plans to gradually increase the capacity of the facility.

That's when the Shasta-Trinity National Forest called for bids to build a new ski resort in the area that had been home to the old Mt. Shasta Ski Bowl, which had since shut down.

The bid was awarded to Carl and Mt. Shasta Ski Area, Inc., so he moved to Mount Shasta and worked full-time on the project. His plans include the construction of seven lifts, three base lodges, and other necessary infrastructure.

In the past 10 years there have been appeals, lawsuits, and further environmental and cultural studies conducted on the project, and construction has not begun. Carl is currently living and working in Bend, Oregon.

But the delay hasn't dashed his dream.

"I see the ski area as an opportunity to repay Siskiyou County," Carl said. "A lot of people helped me grow up, and I see this as something to give back to the community.

"There's an opportunity for a classy resort—not the biggest by any means, but one the community can be proud of. I envision people coming up to the ski area and being met in the parking lot by ski school staff, who introduce themselves and talk about skiing opportunities.

"They'll see a lodge that's beautifully designed to make things easy for them. They'll be able to hire a guide for the day who will teach

Avalanche Track                    George Stroud

Anthony Colburn

# Charlie Simpson

Siskiyou County Sheriff's lieutenant Charlie Simpson has a file like no other in the county: it contains official reports of people who have died on Mount Shasta.

There are 39 of them (36 males and 3 females) dating back to 1916. The first recorded fatality was a pastor from Dunsmuir who was hit by a falling rock which he tried to let roll between his legs. Others have slipped down glaciers, disappeared in crevasses, frozen to death in snowstorms, been buried in avalanches, and suffered heart attacks. Three died in airplane wrecks, and one crashed his hang glider on the Whitney Glacier.

Charlie is chagrined that he was involved in more body retrievals than live rescues during the period between 1989 and 1994, when he served as the county's search and rescue coordinator. He pretty much fell into the job, and then shaped it into what it is today.

Charlie grew up in Siskiyou County and never thought much about the dangerous aspect of Mount Shasta. His awakening came during a body retrieval operation, when a helicopter dropped him and a sheriff's sergeant at the foot of the Hotlum Glacier. The sergeant wanted Charlie to cross the ice field; Charlie was wearing blue jeans and hiking boots and carried no ice axe. It struck him in that moment that there must be a safer way to operate. His wife, Andy, heartily agreed.

In those days, Charlie relied on assistance from local mountaineers who understood ropes, crampons, glaciers, mountain weather, and the challenges presented by Mount Shasta. Deputies in charge of mountain rescues should have the same equipment and know–how, thought Charlie, but he was met with resistance when he approached the department about it.

So, with his wife's encouragement, Charlie took a glacier workshop from a mountain guiding company and spent his own money on an ice axe, crampons, a rope, and other gear. The workshop was an eye–opener.

Michael Zanger

70

"It scared me," Charlie recalled. "I'd never been up to the big crevasses. They look like little cracks from down here, but you get up there and realize you could throw a house into them, and you can't see the bottom."

In 1988 newly–elected sheriff Charlie Byrd told Charlie Simpson to make a list of what he needed to outfit the department for search and rescue missions on Mount Shasta. Charlie happily spent $6,000, and in 1989 became the official search and rescue coordinator.

"Operations on Mount Shasta are different from anywhere else in the county," he said. "The standard in search and rescue today is that you search at night because the person, hopefully, is not walking around. In the past, you went home when it got dark, and it's still that way on Mount Shasta. You're limited by weather conditions, mountain conditions, and helicopter availability and capability. The time involved to get a rescue team and its equipment to a glacier headwall would normally be two days; with a helicopter you can get them there in 20 minutes."

Anthony Colburn

Another challenge on Mount Shasta is the sheer enormity of it: a climber could be anywhere.

"Where do you start?" Charlie asked. "That's when you start looking for clues. Where is the car? What does their wilderness permit say? Which trailhead did they say they were going to use? Was it their intent to reach the summit? Which way might they have come down? Sometimes family members from other areas can't comprehend how big this mountain is. They don't understand why we don't just go find them."

There are success stories, such as the time in 1987 when two men and a woman—all experienced climbers—slid head over heels down the Hotlum Glacier while roped together. The men broke their pelvises; the woman broke her foot but after spending a night on the mountain was able to hike out to the highway and get help. The men were eventually taken by helicopter to the hospital. Two rescue workers who couldn't be retrieved from the glacier by the helicopter before dark spent a glorious night on the mountain and were airlifted out the next day, which is when Charlie coined the phrase "helicopter camping."

A different kind of success story occurred when the body of a man who disappeared on the mountain in 1978 was found nine years later, in 1987, lying in his sleeping bag next to Clarence King Lake in the crater of Shastina. After all those years, the finding was a relief to family and friends.

And then there are those who have not been found. As of the summer of 1995 there were two bodies still on the mountain. One man disappeared down a crevasse on the Hotlum Glacier in 1987. The other fell down the Konwakiton Glacier and also disappeared in a crevasse in 1994. Rescue workers tried, but could not locate either body.

"As a result of my work I've experienced a growing awareness that the mountain is not this gentle thing it appears to be," said Charlie. "I've gained a lot of respect for it, though I don't consider it a 'killer mountain.' It has killed a lot of people, but are there any mountains this size that haven't?

"It's a lot more dangerous than it looks, I'll tell you that," he said. "It's not a simple walk in the woods. If you're going up there, be prepared and don't go by yourself. That's the biggie—don't go by yourself."

Jane English

71

# Erik Berglund

Erik Berglund, a harp player who has recorded five CDs and performs internationally, can live anywhere on the planet as long as he has a telephone, fax machine, and access to an airport.

He has chosen very consciously to live at the foot of Mount Shasta.

"The first time I came here it felt like paradise, and it still does," said Erik, who moved to the mountain in 1991.

Erik grew up half a continent away near Minneapolis, Minnesota. His father taught at St. Olaf College heading the fine arts department, and his mother directed the community choir. Erik enjoyed a childhood rich in the arts. He sang, played piano and violin, and studied drama, art, and film making. He played violin in his father's orchestra when it toured Norway, and sang in the St. Olaf Choir when it toured the United States and Europe.

After earning a degree from St. Olaf, Erik dove into New York City where he acted in off–off–Broadway plays, composed music and performed in puppet theater, drew portraits, played street music, taught voice lessons and mime, and was part of a folk rock band.

And then he discovered the harp—not the jazz version known better as the harmonica, but the kind of harp the angels play. He studied under Mildred Dilling, who also taught Harpo Marx.

"I would go for a half hour lesson and end up there for hours," Erik said.

At the same time, Erik was deeply involved in the city's spiritual community, and began playing his harp for meditation groups, New Age gatherings, and at workshops. It was at a conference in Banff, Canada that he met a musician who was living in Mount Shasta, and later visited him to make a recording.

That's how he stumbled on paradise.

Erik managed his own move to the mountain in 1991. Mount Shasta is home base while Erik travels the world playing his harp in concerts and conducting healings, a gift he discovered he had while on a journey in the Andes Mountains of South America. He has played in Europe, South America, and Canada, as well as throughout the United States and in "power points" such as the Great Pyramid and Machu Picchu.

"I have played in places that are breathtakingly beautiful, and I've played in many of the world's power points," said Erik. "But there is something special above all the others here in Mount Shasta. That's why I choose to live here.

"It's more than just the beauty," he said. "It's easier to meditate here, and to draw inspiration, and to regroup from whatever I've been doing elsewhere in the world. It feeds me. I can sit at a lake with my harp, see the mountain reflected in the water, and all of these beautiful melodies come to me. The mountain is just this brilliant conductor of creativity."

Erik has recorded many projects in Mount Shasta, at Shasta Song Studios. He has recorded elsewhere—most recently in Germany—but the Mount Shasta venue is his favorite because he can look out the window and see the mountain as he plays his harp and sings.

Erik believes that Mount Shasta manifests many good things.

"I think the mountain is responsible for creating strong unity in the spiritual community here, where it feels like we all work together without competition. It's like a loose–knit family here, and I haven't seen that anywhere else.

"Mount Shasta opens you up to feel reverence for God's creation, for nature, and for all life, from something as big as the mountain to something as small as a dragonfly or wildflower. If we applied the same reverence to all of the people we meet, we'd have a much better world.

"Every place has an energy. I've played inside prisons, and in a prison— even with your eyes closed—you can feel that energy. I've been in places in the Yucatan where people's hearts were cut out, and you can feel that energy.

Jane English

"Mount Shasta has a positive energy that creates an incredible uplifting. It makes people feel good; it makes people smile. That's something visitors say to me about the people who live here, that they're very friendly and smile a lot. I was in a beautiful park in Hungary two days ago, and no one smiled or greeted me.

"I'm very grateful that I can be here. I travel to unusual places, connect with different energies, and meet beautiful people. I go to play my harp, and appreciate where I am, but I'm counting the days until I'm back here in what I consider paradise."

# Floyd Buckskin

*Floyd Buckskin is Headman of the Ajumawi Band, Pit River Tribe whose traditional lands lie east and south of Mount Shasta. He wrote the following about realizing the Creator's purpose in Mount Shasta:*

The mountain is sacred just as all things created by the Creator God are, but are we supposed to worship and glorify the things created above the Creator himself? Where is that love for him?

I love Mount Shasta because the Creator made it just like he created everything. But I love him more because he can help me, teach me, love me. He can heal and correct me. Mount Shasta cannot do that of itself. But the Creator's active spirit through Mount Shasta, through you or anything, or direct from the Creator himself, can.

It is the Creator's active spirit in all of creation that keeps us alive. It is in all of us if we just acknowledge and honor the Creator, worship him in spirit and truth, and throw out the middleman.

The only reason that Mount Shasta is important and any of his creation including you and me, is to remind one another of the Creator, God, and that his purposes will be realized in all of creation, so that honor and worship are directed to him, not to the thing created. I love the Creator, I love you, I love life, I love the earth, there is no need to fight over that. Let the Creator be praised on the mountain, in your home, in your heart, by the river, beneath the shade tree; everywhere at all times and places let him be praised.

No mountain can contain him, no temple, no palace, even the earth, nor the stars, but he contains and maintains them all. He establishes his tents with us, and these things that we are expire and cease to exist before him, but he calls us into being and we exist again, because he loves us, and his will and purpose is realized forever.

Then why protect anything? It's because the Creator gave us a responsibility the day of our creation to take care of the earth. Our people have been here for thousands of years. One of the old prophesies speaks about how we had to take care of this place, take care of this land, take care of this earth, these plants and things, because that's our life. The prophesy says that when the snow begins to disappear on Mount Shasta, we as a people will also disappear. It says that when the snow disappears, things will come upon your people, upon the land, that will threaten your very existence.

That's why we make any effort to protect sacred places, mountains, streams or lakes, animals. We don't own it, the Creator owns it, but he gave it to us to use, to respect and take care of it, until such time as he comes to reclaim it. The earth isn't just the planet, it's you and me. Do we love one another, take care of one another, feed one another? We're not Americans, we're not Europeans, we're not Indians. We're not our own people but his people. The things that belong to him are his. So he is returning to examine us to see if we have fulfilled what he has put us here for. And if we have lived up to that, then we can enter into his joy, his life.

So what does Mount Shasta mean to Native people? It means our culture, our way of life, our food, our religion, our symbols, and all those things like that. It's important to us. And those are for our teaching and our understanding, and they're not necessary for you. You have your teachings and traditions that you can draw on. It's available, it's not hidden anywhere. Eagle feathers aren't necessary to pray, to communicate with the Spirit. We can do that freely, without material things before us. So we can go to the mountains, the rivers, the streams, the quiet places, because the Creator calls us to those quiet places so that we can talk to him without interruption and without confusion. We need these places; that's why we need to take care of them, because we're taking care of our need to be with and communicate with the Creator in a beautiful way.

Bob Dalleske

Mark Gibson

## Carolyn Briody

Other than a mystical, magical presence, Mount Shasta has been more like a beacon for our family.

My husband Greg and I lived in the Bay Area before making the move here. And though we had a nice home, good jobs, good friends and family close by, the "beacon" for us there from our second–story window was the oil refinery smoke billowing out of the smoke stacks.

Life was harried most of the time and tentative at best—commute traffic to contend with, daily newspaper headlines shouting at you "Drive By Shooting" or "Freeway Pile–Up: Two Killed," and a nuclear weapons station only a few miles away.

Something was missing in our lives and we started looking for it.

To "get away from it all" on the weekends required several hours journey in almost any direction, and we found ourselves most often heading north—Mount Shasta being the beacon that shone above the rest.

We were entrenched in the rat race and looking for a way to escape.

Having a young family gave us more impetus to look for a better place to raise children: safer streets, a slower pace of life with more time to enjoy family activities, outdoor recreation nearby, friendly neighbors who knew and cared about each other. We were both brought up in small town communities where childhood memories were good and we wanted the same for our own children.

A nine–year–old boy was murdered in the schoolyard one Saturday (the school our young children were to attend). They never found the murderer or the motive. That pretty much sewed it up for me.

After thoughtful exploration throughout the west we decided that Mount Shasta was "the place" for us. Greg and I were lucky enough to each be granted a year's absence from our jobs and our feeling was that if it was meant to be, things would work out. That was the summer of 1988.

Greg found a job that fall as a Youth Service Specialist for Siskiyou County Schools; I worked as a substitute teacher before giving birth to our third daughter that February. A teaching position followed the next fall and we resigned our Bay Area positions. We've never looked back with a moment's regret.

Mount Shasta is so many things to the so varied people who reside at its base. In my present position as Home Study Coordinator with the Mount Shasta Union School District I encounter people from all walks of life whose philosophies of education and of life continue to educate me daily. To most, it was the mountain that brought them here, be it for spiritual reasons, or environmental, or employment, or reasons similar to ours.

For us, as a family, it was the beacon that signalled a less frantic pace of life, a small town atmosphere, clean air, pure water, a playground unsurpassed for all its beauty, and recreational possibilities. Mount Shasta has been all of that, and more.

Shopping Center—Mount Shasta City                    Jane English

Jane English

As a child, I would stare at the lone wonder of Shasta and identify with her solitude. Now, thousands of miles away in a city surrounded by mountains, I still hear her song. When I am feeling lonely I think back to her, and she tells me it can be beautiful to be alone.

— *Bethany Nelson - Anchorage, AK*

Mount Shasta City                    Jane English

Mountain of my childhood past —
My heart e'er yearns for thee.

Stop a minute,
Turn your head
And blow her a kiss for me!

— *Laura Melo Spinetta*

Jane English

I deeply appreciate being a daughter of this Majestic Mountain.

Having been birthed at the base of this dramatic landscape has spoiled me.

There is no other place to be.

My gratitude evokes a responsibility. I accept.

— *Beverly Shannon*

Predawn Moonlit Mountain    Jane English  →

# Bill Miesse

*Bill Miesse turned a chance encounter with an old painting of Mount Shasta into a decade–long search for hidden documents, maps, books, and artifacts central to the scholarly study of the great mountain's legacies.*

*A resident of the Mount Shasta area since 1981, Bill earned a bachelor's degree in Interdisciplinary Studies from The Evergreen State College in Washington state, and a master's degree in Environmental Education from Humboldt State University. He was also a chemistry major for three years at the University of California at Santa Barbara.*

*Bill's research of Mount Shasta's history led him to write an as–yet–unpublished manuscript titled* The Significance of Mount Shasta as a Visual Resource in 19th and Early 20th Century California: Art and Artists 1841–1941. *He also wrote* Mount Shasta: An Annotated Bibliography, *which was compiled from the Mount Shasta Collection at the College of the Siskiyous Library. He hopes the extensive bibliography, published in 1993 and consisting of more than 1,250 annotated entries, "has helped to in some way rescue from obscurity a multitude of scientific, literary, and artistic contributions by worthy men and women of the past."*

*He is also a lecturer who speaks on the topics of Joaquin Miller, early California cartography, the Wilkes Expedition, Mount Shasta's literature, and Mount Shasta's art legacy. His interest is in "using the history of the mountain as a means of connecting us as residents of Mount Shasta into the great traditions of art and science of the world."*

*Here is the story of Bill's search for the first non–Native American image of Mount Shasta.*

In 1986 I bought a painting of Mount Shasta in a local antique store. It was by an artist named Alphonso Broad, and it was signed, but not dated. It had a peculiar quality to it. You could almost feel the tree bark and the distant fog at the foot of the snow–covered mountain. I brought it home and found myself experiencing the tangible feeling of it; it wasn't all visual. All of a sudden I realized that this was a beautiful, priceless piece. It was a timeless thing, and it gave me an amazing thrill which I'd never experienced before.

Naively, I assumed that maybe it was the earliest painting that had ever been made of Mount Shasta; I felt compelled to find that out. I began by studying paintings in galleries and antique stores in the region, and then came upon a surprising twist: the farther away you get from Mount Shasta, the more paintings there are of the mountain. That's true because the art that was produced of Mount Shasta was created, and then purchased, by people from outside the area. A painting of Mount Shasta even won first place in an art show in Vienna, Austria at the turn of the century.

As I spent time in antique shops, I started looking at old books, and sometimes I'd find an engraving of Mount Shasta. That happened to me a hundred times or more. So I became aware that books had the earliest pictures. I wanted to find the first image of Mount Shasta, whether it was photography or some kind of artwork.

I finally came across an old book in an antique store in San Francisco that included an engraving which I believe is the oldest image of Mount Shasta. This picture, called "Shasty Peak," was drawn by artist Alfred Thomas Agate in 1841 and was first published in 1844 as a full–page steel engraving in the five volume report by Charles Wilkes, commander of the United States Exploring Expedition of 1838–1842.

Agate's first–hand view of "Shasty Peak" is a scientific drawing which records the observations of the expedition's scientists, and shows many things of interest: two Native Americans of the Shaste tribe dressed in skins and one holding a bow and wearing

Jane English

80

Pan Brian Paine

an arrow quiver; accurate renditions of Ponderosa and Sugar Pine trees; a demonstration of the grand size of a tree trunk in scale to the Native Americans standing on it; the characteristically shallow root system of a grand conifer fallen over; and, of course, the mountain itself, in what is a reasonably accurate view of the summits of the mountain as seen from the foothills of Mount Eddy, due west of Mount Shasta.

As for the oldest painting of the mountain, in a bona–fide locatable sense both an 1863 Albert Bierstadt oil painting and an 1863 Juan Wandesforde watercolor are the earliest extant original artworks I know about. There is only a fair chance that any earlier paintings exist, though earlier drawings and lithographs certainly exist. For instance, there is an 1855 lithograph by John J. Young, which might have qualified as a painting in its original form before being turned into a lithograph.

When you think about it, going back to 1841, Mount Shasta has a 150–year–old history of art, and I find that fact exciting and worthy of study.

As for the Alphonso Broad painting which started my search, it was done around 1890, disappointingly late in the scheme of things.

# Lyle Schrock

*The Saint Germain Foundation is a religious activity born out of an unusual encounter on the flanks of Mount Shasta in 1930. Called the "I AM" Activity, it now has members around the world, many of whom visit Mount Shasta on an annual basis to attend the "I AM COME!" Pageant, which depicts the life of Christ.*

*Lyle Schrock is vice president of administration and chief executive officer of the Saint Germain Foundation, based in Chicago. Here he writes about that first mysterious encounter, and the special place the mountain holds in the hearts of members.*

In the late 1920's, a Chicago resident named Guy Ballard was sent on government business to the city of Mount Shasta, where he was to spend the next two years. He was enchanted by the mountain, and would take long walks, refreshed by the tranquil domain of peace and inspiration.

One lovely May morning in 1930, he started at daybreak and asked God to direct his path, and by noon was high on the south side of the mountain. The day was warm, and when Mr. Ballard bent beside a sparkling spring to get a cup of water, he felt an Electrifying Current pass through his entire body. Sensing another's presence, he looked around, and behind him stood a man whom he immediately realized was no ordinary person.

The stranger told him, "My Brother, if you will hand me your cup, I will give you a much more refreshing drink than spring water." Although the stranger did not seem to put anything into the cup, it filled with a creamy liquid. The man explained that it came from the universal supply—omnipresent, vivifying life itself.

So began Mr. Ballard's long association with Saint Germain, one of the Great Ascended Masters. For nearly two years he met Saint Germain for daily instruction.

One day, as Mr. Ballard waited on a log for Saint Germain to arrive, he glanced to the side and saw a mountain lion, or panther, slinking stealthily toward him. He became frantic with fear until he remembered Saint Germain's revelations of the previous day; that Life, Omnipresent Life, which exists everywhere about us, is subject to our con-

scious control and direction and is willingly obedient when we love enough, because all of the universe obeys the Law of Love. Mr. Ballard realized that he had the "Mighty Presence of God" within him, and that this magnificent animal was a part of God's life, too. Certainly, he thought, one part of God could not harm another part.

Feeling great love toward the animal, he moved slowly towards it. He saw the mountain lion's eyes soften, and when they met, the animal rubbed its powerful shoulder against Mr. Ballard's leg. Mr. Ballard stooped to stroke its head, and it was at this point that he looked up to see Saint Germain standing beside him.

Saint Germain congratulated him for his courage, and explained that he was in no way responsible for the mountain lion being there, that it was all part of the Inner Operation of the Great Law.

Saint Germain's instruction prepared Guy Ballard for his future role assisting humanity, a role in which he would try to alert the nation to make a concentrated and conscious effort to neutralize the destructive forces that mankind has generated. Mr. Ballard eventually founded the Saint Germain Foundation (the "I AM" Religious Activity), a vast organization with members located all over the world. Under the nom de plume of Godfre Ray King, he also wrote a series of books including *Unveiled Mysteries*, *The Magic Presence*, and *The "I AM" Discourses*.

The Activity maintains headquarters in Chicago, and has a beautiful retreat called Shasta Springs near Mount Shasta. Special reverence is given to

Mount Shasta by members because it was on its slopes that their founder met Saint Germain. Every year on the second Sunday in August, in the beautiful Guy W. Ballard Amphitheater at the foot of the mountain, an outdoor pageant on the life of Christ is held. Many of our members look forward to coming to Mount Shasta every year, for it is under the radiation of this great giant of nature that one receives inspiration and spiritual renewal.

About three times a year I leave the office in Chicago to stay at Shasta Springs near Mount Shasta. If I fly into San Francisco, I watch for the mountain from the plane. When I drive north, I usually see it from Red Bluff and that's a real treat. Being near the mountain is truly inspiring. It's kind of a second home for me.

I AM Pageant                                    Michael Zanger

Jane English

# Charlie Byrd

*Charlie Byrd, California's first elected African-American sheriff, was born in Weed in 1947. In the early 1940's his mother had traveled alone by train from Louisiana to California to join her sister and work in the Weed Laundry. Charlie's father came from Mississippi about the same time to work on the pipefitters crew at Long Bell Lumber Company, also in Weed.*

*Charlie went to Weed schools and also worked in the laundry part-time and on weekends doing cleanup chores until he was 18. He then worked as a patcher and plugger at the International Paper Company plywood plant in Weed for three years while taking classes at College of the Siskiyous.*

*He was hired part-time in the Weed Police Department in 1967 and worked his way up the ranks until he was named chief in 1975. After a successful countywide campaign, he was sworn in as sheriff of Siskiyou County on January 5, 1987, and was re-elected to begin another four-year term in 1991.*

*Here's how the county sheriff views Mount Shasta.*

When I became sheriff I got a different perspective on that mountain: I have to deal with it rather than kick back and enjoy it. People get lost, people get hurt, people get killed up there. It's a major factor in storms. There's political controversy around it.

I also think of Mt. Shasta as a problem because it's a volcano. When Mt. St. Helens erupted, the sheriff in that county had fits. People don't accept that Mt. Shasta is going to erupt, but someday it's going to do that. We'll be trying to convince people to leave once we see the warning signs. We'll have to have an aggressive educational program going with the first signs of an eruption.

The sheriff is the chief law enforcement officer in the county so we'll be the ones to invoke mutual aid from departments outside the county to help with an evacuation.

West from Little Mt. Hoffman    Jane English

Jane English

Depending on where the eruption actually occurs, we'll evacuate to the north or south. Some sides of the mountain would create more problems than others in that sense because of where the populated areas are. Then we'd have to protect the land and property once everyone was gone.

When it does erupt, the glaciers will melt and we'll probably have problems with flooding, besides the problems with lava and ash. We'll also have a problem with wildland fires.

After Mt. St. Helens erupted, I attended U.S. Geologic Survey workshops that gave instructions on how to try to handle all the problems that come with the evacuation and eruption.

Aside from the 'problem' aspect of Mt. Shasta, I do appreciate it. I've hunted up there a lot. I've hunted every side of the mountain with the exception of the McCloud side. It's good hunting. If you see a buck, you know it's going to be a good one. Big bucks stay high; it's cooler and it's safer for them.

I've snowmobiled up there, but I haven't skied. Even though I was born and raised here I never got involved in the ski school programs. I think my parents were afraid of having me ride on a school bus on the mountain because they came from the South where there was no snow, and they didn't ski. Blacks weren't into skiing. They're still not.

When I don't see the mountain, I miss it. I wonder how much snow is up there and what's going on with the weather. I've seen the dust from rock slides in the summertime. When the glaciers melt and Whitney Creek starts to flow, that's really impressive. I'm also impressed with Shastina, that the top of the cone is gone. I visualize how much dirt was blown out and where it all went.

There's nothing spiritual about that mountain, though.

Sunrise

# Jerald Jackson

When Jerald Jackson talks about "The War," you have to clear your mind of tanks, aircraft carriers, and other World War II images.

Jerald's war—his people's war—was the Modoc War in 1873, a series of bloody battles which pitted Modoc Indians against the United States Cavalry. The fighting took place at Captain Jack's Stronghold, which is now part of Lava Beds National Monument on the northeast side of Mount Shasta.

Jerald remembers being taken out to the battle site as a young child by his great–great–grandmother and her sister.

"I was holding their hands as we looked out over Lava Beds, and they pointed and said, 'This is where our people fought a war,'" Jerald said.

It is also near where the Modocs believe they were created. Their land of creation was not on Mount Shasta, a landmark which figures into some other Native American creation beliefs. But the snow–covered mountain on the horizon does have some significance to the Modocs, and, in a very personal way, to Jerald Jackson.

Jerald, who lives in Klamath Falls, Oregon, was born in 1938 in the Klamath Indian Agency Hospital on what was then the Klamath Reservation. (In 1954, the reservation was terminated along with federal recognition of the three tribes that make up the Klamath Tribes: Klamath, Modoc, and Yahooskin Band of Snake Indians. Federal recognition has since been restored, but the 1.2 million acre reservation has not; the Klamath Tribes have no land base.)

Jerald was raised by his great–great–grandmother Anna May Copperfield Riddle because Jerald's father left when he was a child, and his mother was an alcoholic.

Anna May kept Jerald at a place called Whiskey Creek until he was 7, and then moved to Bonanza, which she told him was their true home. Bonanza is where Jerald went to public school.

"It was pretty harsh," he remembers. "I didn't know how to speak English very well. The kids made fun of me because I was dark, and overweight, and didn't speak well. I was beat up a lot. I can still feel that in me."

He was also schooled by Anna May, who taught him what he refers to as "Indian values."

"Being honest, being brave, believing in God, respecting yourself and others," he said. "I believe I am just here for a journey. My body might be from here, but I'm not from here. This land doesn't belong to me; I belong to it. Everything created by the Creator has a purpose."

In his early teens, Jerald separated himself from Indian values and got involved with alcohol, drugs, and the law. He was sent to Oklahoma to be with a cousin, but the situation only got worse. When Jerald returned to Oregon to live, the scoldings from the elders were so harsh that he would cross the street to avoid them.

On July 15, 1975, he made the decision to stop drinking, and joined Alcoholics Anonymous. He also sought the help of a counselor at the Klamath Alcohol and Drug Abuse Center, which is where Jerald works as a counselor today.

Two vision quests, both in the area of Lava Beds National Monument, have helped him to reunite with his own spiritual nature. Eddie White Wolf, the medicine man, or shaman, who helped Jerald with his first vision quest, later died of a heart attack in Jerald's arms after helping another man begin a vision quest. The second shaman to help Jerald, Stanley Smart, has also passed away.

But they taught Jerald to know his spirit helpers, certain animals and winged creatures which Jerald considers to be his relatives. Helpful to him are deer, bear, hummingbirds, and eagles.

Mule Deer at Lava Beds      Jeffrey Rich

"I was instructed to pay attention to what direction eagles come to me from," said Jerald. "From the north is purification, east is vision, west is to look within myself, and south is trust. I also pay attention to what direction the eagles leave in."

Anna May, Jerald's first instructor, told him that Mount Shasta was "a boundary line," and that there would always be safe passage between Mount Shasta and Medicine Lake.

"The mountain protected the passage because we believe there are spirits there and they didn't want us warring against each other at that time," he said.

"For me, personally, Mount Shasta is very powerful in the medicine world, and spirit world," Jerald said. "I see it every day; I can feel it. It gives me a good feeling and good energy every time I go near it. Other Indians may not see it the way I do. Not all Indians see things the same way or feel about things the same way. But Mount Shasta makes me feel humble every time I'm near it. I think that there is a Great Spirit there."

Tule Lake          Larry Turner →

Hawk Chick       Jeffrey Rich

Quail       Jeffrey Rich

Owl       Jeffrey Rich

Bald Eagle       Jeffrey Rich

Cottontail Rabbit       Jeffrey Rich

Long before
humans lived near
Mount Shasta,
animals of many kinds
made their homes
on and around
the mountain.

Tiger Swallowtail       Jane English

Porcupine       Frank Kratofil

Mountain Lion       Jeffrey Rich

Pronghorn Antelope       Jeffrey Rich

Hummingbird                    Jeffrey Rich

Osprey                         Jeffrey Rich

Mountain Bluebird              Jeffrey Rich

Mule Deer                      Frank Kratofil

Snow Geese                     Larry Turner

Black Bear                     Jeffrey Rich

Frog                           Jane English

Striped Skunk                  Jeffrey Rich

Yellow-bellied Marmot          Jeffrey Rich

89

# Jackie Young

*Jackie Young lives half a world away from Mount Shasta, in London, England, yet she feels the mountain's presence constantly and her experiences there have had a deep and abiding influence on her life.*

*Jackie has physically visited the mountain once, during a week–long spiritual retreat in 1992, but her connection with it remains strong. Pictures of Mount Shasta adorn her home along with pictures of other mountains and sacred sites.*

*After she trained as a clinical psychologist and completed her undergraduate and master's degrees in England, Jackie worked for the National Health Service there. In 1981 she went to Japan for a three–week vacation and ended up staying there for five years training in oriental medicine and parapsychology, and doing intense spiritual practice with Japanese, Chinese, and Tibetan teachers. It was in Japan that she met the teacher who was to draw her to Mount Shasta almost 10 years later.*

*On her return to England in 1985 she helped to establish two integrated clinics for women and has gone on to specialize in complementary and alternative medicine. She now teaches, lectures, writes, and broadcasts in this field, and runs a health assessment practice. At the same time she maintains her interest in personal and spiritual development and makes regular visits to India.*

*These are her thoughts on the mountain:*

I first saw Mount Shasta on a postcard I received in the late 1980's and immediately felt its magnetic pull, its beauty, its majesty, and its mystery. I longed to go there and inwardly prayed that one day I would visit.

The invite to go to Mount Shasta came when I visited California in the summer of 1992. A beautiful and very special spiritual teacher, Dolores Hand, who was born Hong Kong Chinese but naturalized American, was running her annual retreat there and invited me to join. I had met Dolores in Japan and knew of her spiritual gifts and her work in many countries. I decided to go.

I arrived in Mount Shasta City at night and couldn't see the mountain. We rose at four o'clock the next morning to climb to a plateau partway up the mountain for morning meditation as a group. I still couldn't see the mountain as it was still dark, but I could feel it. I could feel its fantastic power, its strength, its depth, and its promise, and my heart was singing as I climbed; fatigue disappeared with every step.

The morning meditations were magical as we sat in silence until dawn crept over the mountain. Later we chanted and sang and listened to words of wisdom from our teacher before descending. Dolores always described the mountain as one of the most sacred places on earth, and always treated it with the utmost respect.

Before speaking to us she would stand motionless, transfixed on the mountain's peaks, tuning in to the mountain and communing with the deities that she said abided there. On two mornings, as we completed our meditations, we were blessed with wondrous rainbows spanning the sky alongside the mountain. Once it was a double rainbow—something I had never seen before, or since. The beauty of it took my breath away.

Squaw Valley Creek      Audra Gibson

Every afternoon we gathered for teachings in a clearing amongst the lofty pines at the base of the mountain. Sitting amongst these spectacular, aged trees was a complete contrast to being high up on the sparse rock for the morning meditations

In amongst the trees Dolores gave us teachings on a wide range of spiritual subjects and occasionally led us on a guided meditation. The most memorable one for me was one which led us inside the mountain itself. She had told us that it was possible to go inside the mountain, but not all could achieve this; that the mountain was a repository of numerous spiritual secrets revealed to individuals only as it was appropriate.

In the meditation we traveled high up the mountain in our mind's eye and had to find a "door" in the mountainside to get in. I was skeptical of my ability to do this and was expecting nothing to happen when all at once, to my amazement, a door appeared in the rock face and I was able to go inside! It is almost as if the inside of the mountain exists on another plane of being.

It is not solid; it is filled with light chambers and in each it is possible to get answers to questions and gain access to immense wisdom and knowledge.

I learned things in there that have informed my life ever since, and the experience transformed my view of the mountain. After that I could no longer view it as solid; I felt as if I could literally walk through it and be on, or in, any part of it at any time. That is why I can feel as if I live on the mountain even though I am thousands of miles away. In my mind's eye I can be on the mountain any time I like and at the same time it is always here with me.

I think the mountain has given many people spiritual insights whether they are climbing, skiing, or just looking at it. That is one example of its power.

In the same week that I was asked to write about Mount Shasta for this book, I also learned that Dolores had died. I am filled with love and gratitude to Dolores and to Mount Shasta for all I learned there.

I feel privileged to have set foot on the mountain and shared in its magnificence. Shasta is a very sacred and holy mountain and all whose lives are touched by it are fortunate. I was three months pregnant with my first and only child when I joined the retreat on Mount Shasta, and I feel he, too, was blessed and energized by this wondrous mountain. I hope to return with him one day to give thanks.

Jane English

# Jack Carman

**W**hen Jack Carman was eight years old, he ventured to the edge of his family's farm near Tulelake and made a circle of rocks on top of a small rise.

"It was my personal place to go," said Jack, now 43. "When I was there, Mount Shasta was the biggest thing on the horizon to look at. It was a good focal point for daydreaming."

Jack's father is a World War II veteran who was awarded the 72–acre homestead on the mountain's northeast side in 1948. He used the land to grow barley and wheat. Before that, as a young man, he operated a dairy and orange groves in Southern California.

In 1952, Jack was born in the nearest big city—Klamath Falls, Oregon. And so began his life in the country.

"It was a really simple, uncomplicated, hard–working life," Jack recalls. "I remember lots of hiking, spending time in the fields, chasing Dad on the tractor like I was a dog. That was excitement for me."

And then there was his rock circle.

"Any child who grows up here has such broad horizons," Jack said. "I learned to be contemplative. I spent a lot of time just looking out across the landscape."

Jack attended local schools and then left home to attend the California State University at Fresno, where he majored in English and philosophy and

earned a teaching credential. Two years before graduating he married Shelley Breuer, who also majored in English and earned a teaching credential.

In their early dating days, Shelley listened as Jack spoke to her of the farm, the vastness of the land—and Mount Shasta. It didn't take too many visits to the area for her to fall in love with it, and to miss seeing Mount Shasta when she headed back to Fresno.

Jack didn't expect to become a farmer, but in 1975 he and Shelley moved back to Tulelake to help on the farm where Jack's parents live, as well as an additional 150 acres that the family had purchased earlier. (They've since sold the larger parcel, though Jack and Shelley still live on the land, and Jack teaches at a continuation high school in Tulelake.)

"Back then we raised hay, grain, sugar beets, and children," said Jack, referring to daughter Arin and son Adam. Jack and Shelley preferred to bring their children up in a simple setting with a strong connection to the earth, but things have changed somewhat: computers, books, jazz, and classical music are a part of life for Arin and Adam.

As is the case with their parents, Arin and Adam also spend time watching the dawns, the storms, and the sunsets on Mount Shasta.

"Farmers spend a lot of time going back and forth, three to six miles an hour, in half–mile stretches from one end of the field to the other," said Jack. "When you're doing something that repetitious, it's a pleasure to have something on the horizon like Mount Shasta to focus on."

Shelley said that watching the clouds and colors change on Mount Shasta would give her something to do while working in the fields. A clear image in Jack's mind is that of baling hay on full moon nights and watching geese, egrets, cranes, and owls silhouetted against the white mass of Mount Shasta which seemed to glow from within.

Although he grew up in sight of the mountain, Jack was never interested in climbing it—until 1990, when he couldn't get the idea out of his head. As Shelley put it, the two became obsessed with climbing Mount Shasta.

"But I was a little afraid that climbing the mountain would shatter the mystique I feel from this side of it," said Jack.

Still, they climbed. Shelley made it to Red Banks at 13,000 feet. Jack climbed to the summit. The accomplishment, he said, did not diminish the mountain's mystique.

"It's almost as if there are two mountains—the one I climbed, and the one I look at from here," he said. "I have a fuller experience of the mountain now. I can look at it and say I've been to the top of it, but I don't think about that every time. It's a Zen experience, really, because it's one I prefer not to put into words."

Larry Turner

John Jackson →

# Gary Zukav

*Gary Zukav is a writer who lives within view of Mount Shasta and prefers to make his summit climbs by the light of a full moon.*

*He is the author of* The Dancing Wu Li Masters; An Overview of the New Physics, *winner of The American Book Award for Science in 1979, and* The Seat of the Soul, *a national bestseller. His books have sold over a million copies and have been translated into 14 languages.*

*Gary graduated from Harvard with a degree in International Relations, and was a Special Forces officer in the United States Army with Vietnam service. He lectures internationally on consciousness, evolution, and the soul.*

*He was interviewed at his home on Mount Shasta.*

**Q**: How is Mount Shasta a symbol of the ideas expressed in your books, and in your work–in–progress?

**A**: Mount Shasta, to me, is a symbol of the greatness in each of us. Each of us relates to Mount Shasta as we relate to ourselves. If we cannot see the greatness in ourselves, we cannot see it in Mount Shasta, either. If we're brutal to ourselves—the way we think, the way we speak to ourselves inside—then we are brutal to this mountain. If we appreciate ourselves as magnificent Beings in a magnificent living Universe, a Universe of beauty and Life, then we will treat Mount Shasta the same way.

Bobbie Richardson

**Q**: How would people who are brutal to themselves be brutal to the mountain?

**A**: They would exploit it. They are not sensitive to the mountain's physical beauty, or its place in this magnificent ecology, just as they are not aware of themselves as magnificent Beings, or their importance in an interlocking system of Life. A person is brutal to himself if he cannot appreciate and forgive himself, if she condemns herself and cannot see that she is a Being striving to express her potential more fully and beautifully.

We should ask ourselves, do we treat this Earth as a sacred, living Being? Or do we treat it as an inert geological formation created by random circumstances, impervious to our actions?

**Q**: Is Mount Shasta more sacred than other places on Earth?

**A**: I feel it is different than elsewhere. I love mountains and have lived in them for much of my adult life. Before I came to Mount Shasta I loved mountains for their visual majesty, clean air, and the way that I felt when I was in them. But I experience Mount Shasta differently. It has become very special to me. When I came here I didn't know that Mount Shasta would affect me so much; I didn't know what a treasure was awaiting me. But I do now.

Please understand that I'm not saying that Mount Shasta is more sacred than any other place on the Earth. It cannot be, because the Earth is sacred; the entire Earth is sacred. This is important to understand.

Everyone that you meet is sacred and yet you are drawn to some more than to others. All are great souls, but the perception of some individuals is more limited than the perception of others. Some see only their own needs. Others have a more expansive energy and we're drawn to them. For me, Mount Shasta is like that. Just as I can say that all of life is sacred, yet Gandhi was a great soul among great souls, I can say that all of Earth is sacred, and Mount Shasta is special.

**Q**: You climb and ski. What role does the mountain play in that sense?

**A**: I use the mountain for recreation. Recreation means to re–create. What I re–create in me when I am on the mountain is inner peace, my appreciation for being alive. I become wholesome again. I slow down. Important and unimportant things separate themselves.

**Q**: Please share an experience from one of your climbs.

**A**: Once I climbed the mountain with a friend, and the weather that day was beautiful. When we reached the summit the air was warm, the sky was blue, and we could see to the horizon. I posed for a few macho pictures, but that didn't feel right to me. So I sat on the summit with my hands on my knees and I closed my eyes. Slowly I could feel my hands begin to drift upwards, without any effort on my part, and I realized that, before this happened, I was appreciating what a very special place the summit is. But what I saw with my eyes closed, and with my hands reaching upward, was that *every* place is The Summit.

**Q**: What would you say to all people, from all walks of life, about their own relationship with Mount Shasta?

**A**: We should treat The Mountain with reverence, the same way we should treat ourselves and each other and the Earth. How else would you treat a great living Being—the Earth—that has nurtured you from your birth, that has given you everything you need to live, that nourishes you and supports you, and asks nothing in return?

Love the Earth as you love yourself. Love this mountain as you love yourself and let your perception of The Mountain teach you about how much, or how little, love you have for yourself.

Jane English

# Fletcher Hoyt

*Berkeley native Fletcher Hoyt moved to Mount Shasta with his parents in 1947, when he was 21 years old. He left to earn a bachelor's degree in animal husbandry, a secondary teaching credential, and a master's degree in agricultural education at the University of California at Davis, and then moved back permanently. Hoyt, 69, and his wife Evelyn breed ostriches in Mount Shasta.*

*A figure skater, skier, mountaineer, and rock climber credited with the first ascent of several climbs in Yosemite, he was once part of an expedition team scheduled to climb Mount Everest, the world's highest peak, but broke his leg before the trip began.*

*He has spent time on Mount Shasta as a rescue worker, as a College of the Siskiyous biology and forestry instructor leading field trips, and as a lover of the outdoors. He recalls when, on skis, he carried his 7–year–old son on his back from Avalanche Gulch to Bunny Flat after the boy broke his leg on a climbing trip. He also remembers the time when his rescue party was called back halfway up the Whitney Glacier because the "victim" they sought was not lost after all, but was instead speaking face to face with the sheriff in Yreka. "I asked the dispatcher to call my wife and tell her we'd been on a wild goose chase, so would she please prepare the goose I had in the freezer," he laughs. "We fed everyone wild goose that night."*

*Some of Fletcher's fondest memories, however, are of his ski descents from the summit of Mount Shasta.*

I made five ski descents from the top of Mount Shasta, twice actually standing on skis next to the summit register. Most of the descents were on the Horse Camp side, but two were on the east side down the Hotlum Glacier and East Hotlum Cirque. When we skied the east side, we'd jump the bergshrund, or glacier headwall. It put you in the air and stretched out 20 feet, with a 12 foot vertical drop.

One of my more memorable ski descents was in 1947 with a group organized by California State University at Chico. Among those on the climb were two Norweigans and two Swedes. Most of the group turned back at Red Banks, but the five us forged ahead.

Conditions were hairy. Ninety mile per hour winds were blowing off the top. When a blast hit from the Whitney Glacier you had to throw yourself down over your skis just to stay on the mountain. We were weightless.

We went to the register book on the summit, but didn't actually ski back down from that exact spot. Instead, we took off a little lower down. On the way down, one of the Swedes tipped off at the left of the Red Banks, down a 50 degree slope over a cornice. I stood there watching him, very impressed, and I figured that if he could do it, then so could I.

As I watched him, I noticed that he never once turned, and because of that he started to get significantly ahead of me. I thought he was crazy. I was thinking, "We can't do this like a straight arrow." He did some long sweeping turns, but didn't slow down much at all.

We made it from the bottom of Misery Hill to Lake Helen in three minutes. For those who aren't familiar with the terrain, let's just say that's very, very fast. We never stopped. It was like skiing on a billiard table, too, because it was that smooth. I had never experienced terminal velocity with that degree of security in all of my skiing experience. It was totally without the constraints of fear. My brother later described watching the snow plumes through binoculars, and said the Swede and I looked like two bodies almost in freefall.

After resting at Lake Helen the Swede said he'd head straight for the Horse Camp lodge from Lake Helen. I thought, 'Be my guest, but I'm going to make a few turns between here and there.' I knew there was a good chance of hitting breakable crust, which is a great way to break your leg.

Anthony Colburn

As I skied I saw these two straight lines at Spring Hill. They looked like someone had put them there with a transit. Then I came to a section where the line was beaten up for about 100 yards, and then went straight again.

It turned out that the Swede had fallen, broken a ski tip, and then continued on despite the damage. But the line was still straight. When we got to Horse Camp I lent him a spare ski tip that I had for the rest of the trip down to Bunny Flat.

Mount Shasta is a place I've enjoyed being. If you've climbed it, then you know it intimately when you look up at it. It isn't like a tourist looking at it; you know intimately the contours that you're looking at.

I made the decision to live here permanently on a return trip to Davis in my 20's. I was heading south on a bus near Dunsmuir and looked back to see the ridgeline to the Eddies, and although I couldn't see Mt. Shasta, I knew where it was.

That's when I thought to myself, "I'm not leaving."

Near Horse Camp          Jane English  →

Mount Shasta is a small quiet place from which to look at yourself. And the mountain is always there when you need to talk to God.

— *Marjorie Stearns*

George Stroud

Mount Shasta is a place of perspective, clarity and spiritual awareness, a beacon of peace, love and light energy. It is the majestic physical manifestation of the archetypal sacred mountain.

— *Ron Otrin*

Castle Lake                                    Michael Zanger

People need to go to that source and find out what the Indians are saying when they speak of the mountain as being a spiritual mountain.

— *Marvin Stevens*
Kickapoo of Oklahoma

Anthony Colburn →

# *Bruce Barnes*

It all started with fly fishing.

When I was a kid growing up in Arkansas, my dad and grandfather were among the minority of people who fly fished there. They taught me what they knew, and I loved it. When I became an adult I got away from fly fishing—until I hooked up with two colleagues at the Bay Area laboratory where I worked. The three of us had experienced no–fishing spells in our lives, and we all wanted to get back into it.

About 15 years ago we started making fishing trips to the Dunsmuir area where one of their dads had taken him as a boy. We'd camp at Castle Crags State Park and then fish local lakes and rivers. From the start I was taken with the beauty of the surroundings.

One night we got tired of cooking and eating our own fish, so we headed to the town of Mount Shasta for dinner. We enjoyed a good Italian meal. It was an autumn evening, just at dusk, and we drove along the main street and through some of the older neighborhoods.

The town had this feel to it that I liked very much. It felt the right size, the right speed, had the right temperament and the right amenities. It just fit, and I decided to trust my gut.

My wife Nancy and I were disenchanted with living in the Bay Area. We were horrified by the graffiti and the violence. We'd already started planning an early retirement and were building an "escape" fund. I was just lit up by Mount Shasta, and when I returned from that fishing trip I told Nancy I'd found the town we were looking for.

The next weekend we returned to Mount Shasta and stayed in a motel. We drove around and walked through some of the neighborhoods, taking it all in. I remember walking along a street and kicking sycamore leaves, dreaming of what it would be like to live there. It was a nice clean area and it seemed to embody the values we had picked up living in the Midwest.

Nancy said fine, let's move here. That was 12 years ago. We started making more trips to the area to fish and stay in a friend's cabin. We organized a retreat here for some of our church members.

On one 10–day trip in 1991, at the point that we were very dreamy–eyed and sappy on the area, Nancy and I went fishing together at Lakin Dam near McCloud. We were sitting at a picnic table and decided to play devil's advocate by making a list of all the reasons we couldn't move here: not much to do, don't know anyone, winters are difficult, can't afford it, and so on.

At about that time, along came an older man and his grandson. The young man went to fish, but the older man came and sat with us. In our conversation we learned that he had moved to McCloud to retire, and that he never regretted his decision. We told him of our reservations and he systematically knocked off every one of them. I don't believe in spiritual things like this, but he was like an angel who came just at the right time.

After he left, Nancy and I looked at each other and said, "What are we waiting for? What else do we need?" We threw our rods in the car, drove back to town, and went to see a realtor. Later we bought a house that we rented out for a year. I retired at age 56 and we moved here July 30, 1993. It's the best thing we ever did.

As for the mountain, I look at it every day, and every evening. I look at it directly or reflected through the windows of our home. I like it when it's rosy, or when it's violet, especially in the fall. I like it when the moon comes up behind it.

Nothing else in these surroundings compares with it; everything else is insignificant. I have to believe there is something significant about Mount Shasta based on the sheer mass of it. The mass exerts some kind of positive, steadying influence. I find it reassuring. I'm not sure if the pure weight of it pulled me, or whether I was just drawn by its size and beauty.

There's something physical about that mountain that I just haven't gotten my mind around.

Jane English

100

Jane English

# Michelle Berditschevsky

*Michelle Berditschevsky is coordinator of the Save Mount Shasta citizen's group, and is secretary of the Native Coalition for Cultural Restoration of Mount Shasta. Both groups seek long term protection of Mount Shasta, and have been active in their opposition to a proposed second ski area on the mountain.*

Mount Shasta is not just another important environmental issue, affecting only the use of natural resources. There are places that coincide with the human striving for sacredness, a deeper dimension, a kinship with all living beings, a place where we can tangibly attune our senses to the Earth's relationship with the holy. This has been Mount Shasta's role from the beginnings of human inhabitation, to which long-standing Native American traditions attest. The Mountain holds a pivotal meaning for our times. At this end of the millennium, when humankind sorely needs a vision of sustainability, Mount Shasta's capacity for taking us to a level where nature still speaks wholly is a safeguard for our sanity, freedom and survival.

The first time I heard about Mount Shasta I knew I would end up here, which finally happened some twenty years ago. My involvement with protection of the Mountain goes back to the summer of 1988, to a particular moment when I was sitting on a ridge high on its western slope. At the time I was writing a book on the perception of nature, a poetic-philosophic treatise on the extraordinary experiences with this Mountain.

On that day progress on the book came to a sudden halt, not another syllable. The open kinship with volcanic rock, white bark pine, the music of wind and water, geological sculptures, and the dynamic relationships of the five life zones that make up this unique ecosystem. . . mysteriously closed. On another stage of my consciousness, an intense spark lit up a vivid drama. It came upon me like a lightning realization through silent voices in the landscape itself—an alarming sense that the mountain's life web was in danger, threatened by a second ski area and likely condominium development. I saw the human forces that jeopardized the Mountain's pristine magnificence, I heard the Indian voices singing by the springs, the legal process to challenge the threat, and the part I could play. In that dynamic instant the whole drama flashed as if I had already lived it—past, present and future merged, and I saw that it could be done, the mountain had to be protected. Many times since I wished I could replay that movie in slow motion—run that one by me again! But there on the ridge, I could only say to myself: "Yes, the world needs this Mountain more than another book."

From that moment on my life changed. I interrupted a seventeen year college teaching career, not another line was added to my book, and the visions and qualities I had experienced on a poetic level resurfaced in the documents we were producing for the case against the proposed ski area. Every time a quality found this new expression, it felt like it was being resuscitated from a dark blanket of forgetfulness and blindsightedness, touching others who were mysteriously drawn into the drama, and attracting, like a magnet, the laws and arguments that could create a sacred space in our human affairs.

The designation of Mount Shasta in its entirety as a Historic District came in March 1994 on the basis of its significance to Native American culture. I feel this recognition that Mount Shasta is vital to the cultural survival of the First People is a step in healing our relationship to them, to the land, to our own souls. Unfortunately, a backlash of forces including ski area proponents, property rights advocates and commercial interests undid much of what took seven years to accomplish, and the Historic District boundaries were reduced up to timberline, eliminating 90% of the designated area from protection. . . .

*against a background*
*white as the soul's beginning*
*figures are drawn into*
*the mountain's pure vortex*
*out of an inner logic*
*that is each player's secret*
*inevitably entering*
*the whirl of events*
*reconfigured by the order*

Pan Brian Paine

*of the heavens it touches*
*this . . . is how much*
*I can give and offer to you*
*beings of space and time who pour*
*vials of justice and seeds*
*from another light*
*into the crucible of the effort*

*heroics . . . like moments of love*
*are snatched*
*from disapproving eyes*
*passion returns after crossing*
*fear's dulled judgment*
*in one inescapable solitude*
*whispers with*
*the only small voice left*

*calling again on the volcano's fire*
*pulsing inside the gleaming stillness*
*veins of molten rock, crystal waters*
*cloud billows, grinding glaciers, dancing sprays of snow*
*resolve into pure white against turquoise blue*
*calling to the Indian who yet roams*
*translucent to the sky*
*of his wild dream*

*my soul was world*
*of that bright silence*
*face suffused in light*
*a spiral breath flew me*
*lighter than a wafting mist*
*to touch the feet of another light*

. . . The effort to preserve Mount Shasta is a microcosm of the issues of the late 20th century—changing views of our relationship to the Earth, the re-emergence of indigenous peoples and more spiritual lifeways, understanding the limits of industry and the need for its integration within a larger living whole. Mount Shasta is the meeting of two world views—technology and dreamtime—the view that seeks to control and subordinate nature to short term needs, and the view which sees in nature and the universe an interconnected life web of mysterious forces and beings to which we are related and with which we can cooperate.

Summit Lake    Michael Monaghan →

## John Signor

*John Signor, an artist and designer living in Dunsmuir, worked as a brakeman for Southern Pacific for 20 years. He has published seven books on western railroad history, including* Rails In the Shadow of Mount Shasta, *published by Howell–North, and his latest release,* Southern Pacific's Coast Line, *published by Signature Press.*

*John wrote the following:*

From the earliest days of the railroad in Siskiyou County, the geographically–prominent peak of Mount Shasta has figured largely in the affairs of the Southern Pacific Railroad. Beginning with the opening of the railroad in 1887, the mountain and the attractions surrounding it, such as "Shasta Springs," were promoted heavily as tourist destinations.

Indeed, the entire route between the San Francisco Bay Area and the Pacific Northwest was known for years as the "Shasta Route." The segment of the railroad between Gerber, California, and Ashland and Crescent Lake, Oregon was designated the "Shasta Division." And a succession of deluxe passenger trains which operated over the route were known variously as the "Shasta," the "Shasta Express," and the "Shasta Flyer." These trains culminated in the "Shasta Daylight," the premier streamliner which operated over the route between 1949 and 1966.

Though desirable from a marketing standpoint, the mountain also presented many impediments to the railroad—and still does. The topography created by this

#4449 - Excursion Train on North Side of Mount Shasta          Jane English

great volcano challenged the railroad builders of the 19th century and imposed steep grades and sharp curvature which complicated railroad operations.

The town of Dunsmuir was founded primarily as a base for helper (pusher) engines which were needed, and still are, to boost the trains over the summit. This in turn fostered the employment of many men who worked on the trains, in the yards, and in the shops which were built to maintain the helper engines.

Weather, generated by the mountain's great height, also affected the railroad. Though not associated with the deep snows that have made other mountain passes famous, serious snowfall has from time to time impeded operations and required the railroad to maintain flangers, spreaders and large rotary snow plows to clear the accumulation from the rails.

Perhaps the most significant aspect of the mountain's weather has been the wind. Upon completion of the Black Butte Cutoff in 1927, the main flow of rail traffic now skirted the very base of Mount Shasta, cutting through lava flows and bridging ravines on its way to Grass Lake and Klamath Falls. And with this new line came a new problem—high winds. On the high trestle at Dry Canyon and in particular the gulch at Bolam, winds of hurricane ferocity would roar down off the mountain and lift trains off the rails. I have seen whole strings of 35–ton rail cars literally blown off the tracks, and the yards at Black Butte are famous system–wide for blizzard–like conditions and the phenomenon of "upside down snowfall."

Northbound Freight                              Kevin Lahey

But as difficult as the mountain can be for the railroad, there are aspects of Mount Shasta from a railroader's perspective that are unique and rewarding.

On the 108 mile run between Dunsmuir and Klamath Falls, Mount Shasta is visible nearly the entire distance from Midland, Oregon, until dropping down into the Sacramento River Canyon at Mott, California. With his business a 24–hour–a–day occupation, the railroader has the opportunity to view the mountain from a variety of angles at all hours of the day and night.

Long trips on the "Black Butte Subdivision" afford the opportunity to view the ever–changing aspects of light, angle, and atmosphere on the mountain. In the Butte Valley near Macdoel, Mount Shasta appears as a glowing peach–colored sentinel on the violet pre–dawn horizon. "In the hole" at Upton at three o'clock in the morning, its snow–covered flanks glisten in the moonlight. On a blustery March day, its summit is shrouded in mystery. But it is the view of Mount Shasta that presents itself when "tipping over" at Grass Lake that is my favorite. Here the mountain looms ominously, dwarfing everything around it, and lit by the long rays of a late afternoon sun, the effect of golden light against a cerulean sky is striking.

It has been some time since I have been "on the road," but the vivid impressions of light on Mount Shasta gleaned from the cab window of a locomotive continue to influence my work.

Sacramento River - North of Dunsmuir

Bob Morris

105

# Michelle Moore

I can't get away from the feeling that I live and work on the "back side" of Mount Shasta, though I'm the first to admit that's an ethnocentric point of view.

But until I went to work for the National Park Service as an interpretive specialist at Lava Beds National Monument, I'd only seen the mountain from along Interstate 5 which runs north to south on the mountain's west side, the side most people know it by.

Every year for the past 15, ever since I was a 12–year–old in San Jose, my father and I have spent a week seeing plays at the Oregon Shakespeare Festival in Ashland, Oregon, just across the California border. We'd get there by way of the coast, camping among the redwoods, and then return home via Interstate 5. As our camper strained its way over Siskiyou Pass, I would catch my first glimpse of Mount Shasta.

At this point I was usually drying my eyes following my annual post–Ashland cry. I was coming out of an intense week of theater and self–examination. I see theater as a very spiritual experience because it can touch you very, very deeply. Ideally, in confronting the issues of the plays, you deal with those issues in yourself. My visits to Ashland with Dad were really pilgrimages that helped shape the person I've become.

Departing Ashland was always difficult and Shasta appeared while I was in a state of emotional transition—half lamenting the end of this special week, half exulting in the challenge of incorporating the truths I'd learned into everyday life. Shasta came to symbolize for me this return to the "real" world, a journey mirroring that of many Shakespearean characters who return to daily urban life having been made more whole by rural or wilderness experiences.

Four and a half years ago I began working at Lava Beds National Monument, a magical, mystical, high desert place covered with lava flows and riddled with caves, and rich in Native American history. Mount Shasta is visible from much of Lava Beds, but for me it's a distant presence. In fact, in my work here, and as an interpreter of this area for visitors, I view Mount Shasta as a rival!

Let me explain:

Here at Lava Beds we're sitting on the largest volcano in the Cascade Range, the Medicine Lake Volcano, yet few people have ever heard of it! It's a shield volcano covering at least 750 square miles, so it's really massive. This volcano is shallow–sloped and dome–shaped, though, so a lot of people don't even realize they're on a volcano. It's very different from Mount Shasta and other famous Cascade volcanos, which I refer to in my campfire programs as being "picture postcard perfect." Visitors to Lava Beds ask me where all the lava in this area came from. They wonder if it's from Mount Shasta. I spend a lot of time explaining that we have our own very wonderful volcano. That's what makes Mount Shasta a rival in my mind.

But I have to admit that it's a beautiful mountain with a presence, even here at Lava Beds. It reminds me of the Grand Canyon which I found overwhelming, almost too big to personalize. In some ways Mount Shasta is the same for me. I have yet to explore its base and have no personal familiarity with the mountain. Maybe I don't feel ready to get to know it yet. Then again, maybe I just haven't gotten around to it.

It's almost like we haven't been introduced, although I blow it a kiss now and then. That tradition stems from Joaquin Miller who wrote this about first seeing Mount Shasta in his book *Life Amongst the Modocs*: "At last I threw a kiss across the sea of clouds, as the red banners and belts of gold streamed from the summit in the long–setting sun, and turned, took up my lariat, mounted, and proceeded down the mountain."

Some of the aura that surrounds Mount Shasta for me is in knowing that it's a sacred place, though I don't profess to understand exactly what that means. We have special places here at Lava Beds that I visit often and that have far deeper personal resonance for me than Mount Shasta.

In my time as a ranger at Lava Beds one lesson I've learned, to slightly misquote Shakepeare's *Hamlet*, is "There are more things in heaven and earth than are dreamt of in my philosophy."

Medicine Lake Volcano and Mount Shasta - from Tule Lake                    Michelle Moore

Tule Lake

Jane English

Michael Monaghan

If Black Butte were not next to Mount Shasta, it would probably be a well-known landmark in its own right. Sometimes when the mountain is hidden by clouds, people driving by on the freeway think Black Butte *is* Mount Shasta!

— *Jane English*

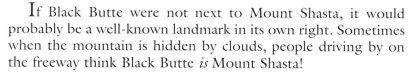

Jane English

John Jackson

Black Butte "borrowing" a cloud from Mount Shasta    Jane English →

# Bruce French

Bruce French and his younger brother Dennis grew up loving Mount Shasta.

Their parents moved to Dunsmuir after graduating from college, and the two boys were born in Siskiyou County—Bruce in Weed in 1947, and Dennis in McCloud two years later.

"My first recollections are of learning to ski on Snowman Hill," says Bruce. "I remember the old rope tow, how heavy and wet it was, and helping the men pack the hill. I remember the ski jump, and the smell of soup and hot chocolate in the stone cabin. Now and then we'd go cross country skiing in the woods."

The family moved to Redding when Bruce was six, but they'd still make frequent trips to the area to camp, fish, ski, and visit grandparents. The visits were less frequent after the family moved farther away still, to Sonoma. In those days the boys were pulled out of school for two weeks during hunting season, and they camped with their father at a favorite site along Swamp Creek on the east side of Mount Shasta.

When Bruce was 14 and Dennis was 12, the brothers climbed the mountain—without their parents.

"We'd done a lot of hiking, so my dad had a lot of faith in us," said Bruce. "We did it in one day from Horse Camp. I can remember how hard it was going up to Red Banks. We found a place where the snow had melted, and sat down away from the wind and cold to have lunch.

Jane English

"We were beat and tired, but other climbers were amazed we'd made it that far and encouraged us to keep going. The rest of the climb was great. The sun hit us after Red Banks and it warmed up. We made the summit

Mount Shasta from McCloud                    Walter Mathison

and signed the register book, feeling very proud of ourselves. Our parents met us at the cabin, and they were proud of us and happy to see us," Bruce remembers.

Over the next 20 years the French brothers made fewer trips to the area, but the mountain still held a special place in their hearts.

Bruce was living in Texas in the spring of 1988, serving as a pilot in the U.S. Air Force. He got a call one day from his mother, who was worried because Dennis was overdue from a skiing trip on Mount Shasta. Dennis was living at a Transcendental Meditation community in Ohio at the time, and had traveled to California to ski the glaciers on the mountain's north side.

Without wasting a minute, Bruce caught the next flight out of Dallas, picked up his mother in a rental car, and the two of them drove to Mount Shasta. The sheriff's department was already on a search.

Bruce and his mother were at the hospital in Mount Shasta when a helicopter lowered onto the landing pad there and delivered the body of Dennis French.

The story goes that Dennis was skiing the Hotlum Glacier when he fell and apparently broke some ribs. He was too injured to ski off the mountain, so he crawled into his sleeping bag and rested on the edge of a snowfield. Between the injury and the freezing temperatures inflicted by a mountain storm, Dennis didn't survive the night.

Rescue crews who found Dennis in his sleeping bag commented on how serene he looked, as though he were just asleep. Bruce suspects that his brother was in deep meditation at the time of his death.

A family friend carried Dennis' ashes to the top of the mountain, and released them in the wind. In that way Dennis joined his father, whose ashes had also been scattered there.

Bruce moved back to the area in 1991 and was eventually hired as general manager of the McCloud Community Services District. In 1992, four years after Dennis died, Bruce climbed Mount Shasta for the first time since he and his younger brother had reached the summit as young teenagers.

"It was the test," said Bruce. "I climbed it to see if there was any change in the way I felt about the mountain after Dennis' death. I respected the mountain and prepared myself well, chose a good time, and went up with a friend. I had a wonderful climb.

"You go through various stages in the grieving process. One of the last stages is what my mother calls 'letting go.' I think that climb was when I was able to let go. It was a time for me to say goodbye. And the mountain was just the mountain, as beautiful as ever.

"Mount Shasta is the epitome of nature as I want to know it. It's something that cannot be conquered, something that no one can call their own. It's something you have to respect."

# Russel Baba & Jeanne Mercer

It strikes Russel Baba as more than a coincidence that he is living at the foot of a spectacular volcano—just as his grandfather did before him.

Russel's volcano is named Shasta, and his grandfather's home was in the rural countryside at the base of Mount Fuji in Japan. Russel was called to his mountain, in some sense, and whether his ancestor was involved is a question that hovers in a conversation like a lenticular cloud.

Russel Baba and his wife Jeanne Mercer are accomplished musicians who moved with their son Masato to Mount Shasta from San Francisco in 1983.

Jeanne had grown up in Anchorage, Alaska and seriously studied the piano. She later attended the San Francisco Art Institute where she majored in painting. It was at a cherry blossom festival in the Bay Area that she discovered taiko drumming, a Japanese style of drumming that is athletic, powerful and spirited.

Beginning in 1972 she studied and performed professionally with San Francisco Taiko Dojo under the direction of Seiichi Tanaka, and that's where she met Russel Baba.

Russel considers his main instrument the saxophone, though he also plays various flutes. A San Francisco native and experimental jazz musician, he was one of the first Asian–American artists to produce and record his own work, "Russel Hisashi Baba," in 1978. His work was critically acclaimed in "Downbeat" and other industry publications.

Over the years Russel performed with violinist Michael White, the late great jazz drummer Eddie Moore, pianist Andrew Hill, and other notable musicians.

But his connection with Jeanne was taiko, and for 10 years they performed with the San Francisco group, touring the United States, Canada, Mexico, Europe, and Japan.

Then came "the call."

For Jeanne, the issue was where to bring up her young son Masato. Remembering her own childhood in what was then the small town of Anchorage convinced her that Masato would be better off in a safer, healthier, rural environment.

For Russel it came down to a choice: place the family, for artistic reasons, into the stimulation of a place like New York City or Tokyo, or spend a year in the country to experience four seasons—and take it from there.

In 1983 they moved to Mount Shasta to be near some close friends, and eventually they bought property and started their own taiko group, Shasta Taiko. For the past 10 years Russel and Jeanne have taught traditional and contemporary taiko, and for eight years have received grants from the California Arts Council under the sponsorship of the Mount Shasta Recreation and Park District, so the lessons are offered for free.

Shasta Taiko has performed at schools, colleges, prisons, hospitals, festivals, arts council presentations, special events, and major taiko concerts in California, Oregon, Nevada, and Alaska. Their local performances draw standing–room–only crowds.

Their philosophy is this: "We believe that one of mankind's higher levels of development is through music, art, and culture; and that cultural exchange and sharing will help to cut through ignorance and fear, helping to attain a higher consciousness for all. In the practice of art and music as a discipline one liberates oneself by developing new skills, discovering different points of view, growing in self–expression, gaining confidence, and creating something to share with others while developing awareness, insight, understanding and compassion."

With that said, Russel allows that the mountain has a subtle, rather than obvious, influence on his music and his life.

"I know it's there, and every day I'm inspired—even when it's cloudy," he said. "But I don't consciously say that a certain piece is a Mount Shasta song. The mountain has a silent massive presence. I strive to attain a kind of presence while playing music—a 'centering' or 'grounding' based on experience, respect, and care—built on a solid foundation, like the mountain."

Pan Brian Paine

"For me the mountain is a constant reminder of how everything is connected," said Jeanne. "Being respectful of such awesome beauty puts one in touch with the ancient spirits and nature spirits, and that comes out in the drumming."

They both remember the mystique of playing taiko on Mount Shasta when Tai Situpa Rinpoche, a Tibetan lama, performed an environmental healing ceremony on the mountain in 1989.

"A group of people hiked partway up the mountain to plant prayer flags," Jeanne said. "Even from that distance, they could hear the rhythm of our drums. That, to me, was very special."

# Phil Holecek

*It would not be wrong to call Phil Holecek a child and student of Mount Shasta.*

*Born in Weed in 1948, he attended local schools and was later accepted by Albertson College of Idaho, where he double-majored in business and sociology and served as captain of the ski team. Phil returned to Mount Shasta in 1971 and went to work in the family clothing business.*

*But skiing was his passion. Phil had learned to love the sport at the Mt. Shasta Ski Bowl, and after it shut down he nurtured a dream to one day build a new ski area on the mountain's slopes. In 1984 he left the store to fully commit himself to the Mt. Shasta Ski Park project. Phil founded, and was named president, of Wintun Development Corporation, a group of local businessmen who, after five years of planning, built the Ski Park on private land. The facility opened to skiers in 1985. It now has two chairlifts and a surface lift, night skiing, and snow making, and entertains over 100,000 skiers each winter.*

*Phil's life changed in 1992 when he was diagnosed with bone marrow cancer. He left the Ski Park at that time and moved to Seattle where he underwent a stem cell transplant at the Fred Hutchinson Cancer Research Center.*

*He and his wife Theresa reside in southern Siskiyou County where Phil hikes, plays guitar, and does volunteer work.*

*Phil wrote the following letter.*

Dear Mount Shasta,

Like other Homo sapiens, who during the past 10,000 years have lived within view of your snow–clad and solitary summit, I call you "The Mountain." I was literally born in your shadow and you have maintained a presence throughout my life much as a parent or grandparent. You are the wise one, the ancient one.

Yet you have many other aspects, many more faces, and they are all beautiful. Your beauty, however, cannot be compared to a mere mortal, but more appropriately to a Goddess. I am taken by your seasonal mood swings, fascinated by your unique ability to control the weather. Your capriciousness appears to be driven by the ever changing light, presenting an unending sequence of charismatic images. Thank you for this daily gift of beauty.

And your power, truly grand though understated. I have felt the bite of your icy winds while kicking my crampons into the side of a glacier, all the while remembering the climbers whose lives you have taken. I have viewed with disbelief the destruction wrought by your powerful avalanches. And I wonder, finally, when your next eruption will occur, as it ultimately will, having done so hundreds of times over your million year lifespan.

Thus you are a teacher. My first lessons were on skis at age 10. You had such an influence with such far reaching effects. Little did I know that you had planted the seeds that would continue to direct my life. My education progressed as I reached your summit during my 16th year, the first of many ascents which would follow during decades to come. As I continued to climb, hike and ski your slopes my knowledge, respect, and love deepened. I fought to protect you while at the same time chasing a dream to bring downhill skiing to your lower slopes. I hope I did the right thing.

For me the learning continues. Today I interpret your lessons as applying to us all, all mankind, all life forms. As I better understand the interconnected nature of life and the physical systems upon which it depends I realize that nature has created invisible balances and links between species and regions of the world. These balances must be respected and maintained if we are to survive.

Thus our respect and treatment of you, Mount Shasta, is an indicator of how we are likely to treat each other and the rest of the planet upon which we all depend for life itself. I am reminded of the famous serenity prayer which reads: God grant me the serenity to accept the things I cannot change, the courage to change the things I can, and the wisdom to know the difference.

Thank you for all you have given me. I am striving to return the favor.

Jane English

Mount Shasta Ski Park          Kevin Lahey →

Cross-culturally and throughout time people have looked to a center, a still point or a world axis for a reference point and a connection to sacred realms that transcend ordinary space and time. For some it is a stone, for some a tree, for some a holy person, for some a quiet, un-nameable place within. Living near Mount Shasta we are constantly reminded of this as the days of our lives circle round the great white stillness.

Larry Turner

Living here at the foot of the mountain it is easy to lose perspective and think this is the center of the universe. In a way it is, as is every other place on earth, and in heaven. But it is good sometimes to see Mount Shasta as a bump in the landscape, simply one place under the sun—an average sized star, in a typical galaxy, in the vastness of space.

— *Jane English*

← Kevin Lahey

117

The mountain is simply and perfectly the mountain.
— *Missi Gillespie*

Jane English

Jane English →

# The Photographers

**Gerhard Bock** is a Sacramento-based landscape photographer who loves to roam northern California in search of the perfect picture.

**Ned Boss** made black-and-white pictures of farm animals on the farm near Mount Shasta where he grew up. He later became a professional photographer, doing wedding, landscape, commercial and sports photography.

**Anthony Colburn** is photography instructor at College of the Siskiyous in Weed, CA. For his master's thesis in art he photographed Mount Shasta, spending much time on the mountain, even sleeping on top.

**Bob Dalleske** is a forester and entomologist who enjoys gardening, ham radio, and gathering data on old-growth forest on Mount Shasta.

**Jane English** began photographing as a child with a box camera given to her by her grandfather who did photography in the early 1900's. *See also page five.*

**Audra** & **Mark Gibson** are full time travel photographers whose photos appear regularly in publications throughout the United States. They make their home in Mount Shasta with their daughter, Shasta Grace and their cat, Cosmo.

**Vada Gipson** is a free-lance writer and photographer who makes her home in Fort Jones, CA.

**Ted Graves** was for 28 years a science teacher at Mount Shasta High School, retiring in 1972. He enjoys hiking the mountains.

**Bob Gray** is a retired forest service employee who has lived near Mount Shasta for nearly fifty years. *See also page 26.*

**John Jackson**, a life-long resident of Siskiyou County, retired to a small ranch in Shasta Valley and has recently begun photographing.

**Frank Kratofil**, a native of northern California, is a chiropracter living in Redding. He enjoys doing wildlife photography.

**Rowena Pattee Kryder** is an author, visionary artist and the founder of Creative Harmonics Institute in Mount Shasta. *See also page 46.*

**Kevin Lahey** is a Mount Shasta-based professional photographer whose images capture the essence of nature and at the same time nurture the spirit.

**Walter Mathison** is a visionary photographer, musician and masseur who lives near Mount Shasta.

**Michael Monaghan** is the proprieter of Boss Photo in Mount Shasta City.

**Michelle Moore** works at Lava Beds National Monument. *See also Page 106.*

**Shari Nordell** got her love of photography from her father and her love of nature from within. She currently lives in Mount Shasta City with her husband.

**Pan Brian Paine** is a British artist, ceramicist, photographer and writer who lives in the Mount Shasta area.

**Phil Rhodes** is a former Mount Shasta area resident and is occasional caretaker of the Sierra Club hut at Horse Camp.

**Jeffrey Rich**, a native of northern California, is a wildlife photographer, a teacher of photography workshops and a science teacher in Shasta, CA.

**Bobbie Richardson** lives in Weed, CA and has been photographing Mount Shasta for 25 years.

**George Stroud**, who currently works as a preserve manager for The Nature Conservancy, is a free-lance photographer whose photographs have appeared in Sierra Club Books, Sunset Magazine and elsewhere.

**Larry Turner** is a professional photographer and writer who was born and raised in Malin, OR.

**Michael Zanger** has for nearly 25 years lived, climbed and photographed Mount Shasta. He is owner of Shasta Mountain Guides and author of *Mount Shasta: History, Legend and Lore.*

Jane English

Prints of many of the photographs in this book are available through the Black Bear Gallery, 201 North Mount Shasta Boulevard, Mount Shasta, CA 96067, (916)926-2334. Custom matting and framing are available for these prints.

Front cover photograph by Jane English    Back cover photograph by John Jackson